D0279512

ARISE

SIR FRANKIE DETTORI

THE BIOGRAPHY OF BRITAIN'S BEST-LOVED
CHAMPION JOCKEY

MARCUS STEAD

JOHN BLAKE

John Blake Publishing
Published by John Blake Publishing Ltd,
3 Bramber Court, 2 Bramber Road,
London W14 9PB, UK

www.blake.co.uk

First published in hardback in 2007

ISBN: 978-1-84454-414-1

British Library Cataloguing-in-Publication Data:
A catalogue record for this book is available from the British Library.

Design by www.envydesign.co.uk

Printed in Great Britain by CPD, Ebbw Vale.

1 3 5 7 9 10 8 6 4 2

Text copyright © Marcus Stead, 2007

Photographs courtesy of Mirrorpix, Action Images, Empics/PA,
Rex Features and Getty Images

Papers used by John Blake Publishing are natural, recyclable
products made from wood grown in sustainable forests.
The manufacturing processes conform to the environmental
regulations of the country

Contents

Prologue

Chances were running out, and Frankie knew it. He was now 36 years old, and questions were being asked about his commitment to riding, whether he was still at the absolute peak of his powers, or perhaps more specifically, whether he still had the will to compete at the very highest level. Younger men were posing a very real threat to Frankie's crown as Britain's leading jockey, their bodies untouched by the years of punishing fasting Frankie's had endured, their lives free from the many outside distractions the Italian had known.

Yet a more complete CV you could not find anywhere in the racing world. Every Classic, every major race from around the world was there, multiple times in many cases. Every major race, that is, except one – the Derby.

Fourteen fabled attempts had been made. Yes, there

are far richer races elsewhere in the world, but this is the one everyone remembers, the one the once-a-year punter sits up and takes notice of, and it was the one glaring omission from Frankie's roll of honour. Even the most casual racing fan knew that Frankie had never won the Derby.

A few weeks before the race, it seemed as though 2007's race would be disappointment number 15. The Godolphin stable seemed to have no obvious contenders for the prize, and their efforts seemed to be geared towards races held later in the season. To the surprise of many, Frankie was offered the chance to ride the Peter Chapple-Hyam trained colt Authorized and, what's more, Sheikh Mohammed released his star jockey for what most would agree is still the world's most famous flat race. It would have been cruel not to, since a Godolphin victory was looking unlikely.

The Derby jinx was always going to be hard to shake off, and the build-up to the race was far from plain sailing. Frankie had battled with his weight in the run-up to the start of the season, an annual obstacle that inevitably gets harder with age. He had a bad knee, and just days before the big race, his son Rocco was taken to hospital with a suspected asthma attack.

Authorized had become the unrivalled favourite once news spread of Frankie being on board. In the hours before the race, you were lucky to get evens, and the eventual starting price was 5-4. The weight of expectation was certainly high. The horse was in perfect shape, and the market agreed this was Frankie's best chance of giving his fans the one prize they so desperately wanted him to capture.

There were some early nerves as Authorized settled well off the pace during the opening stages of the race, as Frankie settled the colt down in the middle of the pack, allowing Kid Mambo to dictate the early pace. This was a marathon, not a sprint. As they approached Tattenham Corner they were tenth, but Frankie knew exactly what he was doing. This was the moment he had waited years for.

He moved to the outside, cruising through the field in the final two furlongs to win emphatically and without any serious threat. A brief moment of wild celebration followed in the weighing room, but by Frankie's standards, it was a subdued victory. He was exhausted by the race, and within minutes he had come back down to earth. A lifetime's ambition, held back by years of cruel fate and bitter disappointment, had finally been fulfilled in a magnificent style none of the 100,000 crowd at Epsom or the millions watching around the world would ever forget.

When he got back to his home in Stetchworth, near Newmarket, he knocked on the doors of all his neighbours and invited them round for a drink. He drank everything he had in the house, then headed for the White Lion in Newmarket, followed by a trip down to the yard to see 'Chapple', before his wife put him in a taxi and sent him home at 1.30am. He needed his sleep – another important day lay ahead.A quick trip over the Channel to ride Jean-Marie Beguign's Lawman in the French equivalent lay ahead. A happy accident led to this opportunity as Olivier Peslier was originally down to ride Lawman, but he had been claimed to ride the appropriately-named No Dream, who finished unplaced. Frankie was still on a high from the previous day, everything was a haze and the adrenaline was still pumping – all this worked to his advantage.

Again, the lead-up to the race was far from perfect when Lawman threw Frankie from the saddle on the way to the start. But come the race itself, allowing for an unsettling false start, things couldn't have gone more smoothly and Frankie made all the running to win the race for the third time.

Frankie had captured the British nation's hearts long before the events of this spectacular weekend in June 2007, but few other sportsmen could dominate the front pages in the days that followed in the way he did. The esteem in which this remarkable man was held had reached new heights. The Dettori star – already fixed in the racing firmament – grew even brighter.

CHAPTER 1

A Second Chance at Life

Frankie Dettori's second life began on a grey summer's day in June 2000. Even before he set foot on the plane, he knew all was not well. The aircraft normally used by the Godolphin stable was being serviced that week, so they had been using a rented six-seater Piper Seneca usually based at Oxford. It would later prove to be an auspicious day for Frankie and his friend and fellow jockey Ray Cochrane, although at the same time it brought great tragedy with the death of regular Godolphin pilot, Patrick Mackey.

Frankie and Patrick had used the plane the previous day and were both unhappy at the way it seemed to judder prior to take off. It had staggered into the air, and then fallen back down again through lack of power, before taking off once more. However, their concerns did not prove enough of a deterrent to stop them taking to the air in the unreliable aircraft the following day.

Despite the heartache this day would bring, it could have been so much worse. That morning, Frankie had called Richard Hills and offered him a lift in the plane to Goodwood, but Hills chose to drive instead. Darley Stud's adviser, John Ferguson, had also turned down a seat on the doomed plane.

Shortly after eleven that morning, Frankie and Ray met up with Patrick at Newmarket. Once on board, Frankie took a seat behind Patrick on the left-hand side of the plane, with Ray sitting next to Frankie near the right-hand window.

The plane accelerated down the grass runway, jerking just as it had done the previous day. As before, it tried to take off before it had the power to do so, jumping a few feet in the air before abruptly hitting the ground. The plane attempted to take off a second time, but again hit the ground with an even bigger thud. On the third attempt it managed to climb a few feet before returning to earth with a nauseating thwack.

Moments later, whilst looking out of his window, Ray saw to his horror that the right propeller and engine of the plane were ruptured. Then smoke and flames began to emerge from the damaged engine. Yet the plane continued its futile attempt to crawl into the sky; it climbed some seventy feet. Then suddenly the broken engine dragged the plane towards Devil's Dyke, the grass bank and ditch that divides the July course from the main racecourse. The tip of the right wing tip of the plane clipped the top of the bank causing it to cartwheel several times before coming to a rest upright amid a shower of sparks just beyond the dyke.

Patrick was unconscious. He never stood a chance. Ray was the first to react, shouting at Frankie to get out before the plane exploded. But Frankie was helpless. The door on his side of the plane was jammed on top of him, and his right leg was hurting too much to move. Blood was streaming down his face, and he thought he may even have been blinded in his right eye.

The two men eventually found an escape route – the door on the baggage hatch was half-open. With Frankie unable to move by himself, Ray had to grab him abruptly by the scruff of the neck, bundle him over the back seat, and throw him through the narrow hatch. Ray knew there wasn't much time, so he hastened his friend's departure with a kick and shove which caused Frankie to land on his broken leg, and left him rolling around in agony on the ground just in front of the tail of the plane.

After a failed attempt to release Patrick, Ray made Frankie's well being his priority and dragged him towards the safety of the dyke. Ray then returned to the plane and forced open the pilot's door in a further attempt to rescue Patrick. No sooner had he done this a fresh explosion from beneath the wing forced him to retreat. Even this was not enough to deter Ray. He took off his jacket to try and beat out the flames, causing him to be burned even more seriously, as he made another attempt to save Patrick's life.

In the end, the intense heat and smoke became too much, and Ray tried entering the plane via the baggage hatch from which he and Frankie had earlier escaped. But by now sixty gallons of fuel had escaped from the ruptured tanks and the plane was an inferno. Ray finally admitted defeat – there was nothing more he could do to save Patrick. Crying and screaming, he went over to join Frankie at the dyke.

Frankie then took out his mobile phone and handed it to Ray who dialled 999. No chances were taken when the ambulance arrived. The two men were tied, somewhat claustrophobically, to stretchers and almost mummified before being lifted onto an army helicopter that had landed nearby.

Taking to the skies again was obviously an uncomfortable experience for Frankie and Ray, but they had little say in the matter, and soon found themselves on their way to Addenbrooke's Hospital in Cambridge.

Within 24 hours Frankie underwent surgery to pin his badly broken ankle and had plastic surgery to repair gashes on his forehead. These operations went astonishingly well and resulted in only the smallest of scars.

Ray got off comparatively lightly, suffering back pains, blurred vision in one eye, and numerous burns on his hands, arms and face. Yet this was to prove enough to end his career. He attempted a brief comeback on 21 July, barely 6 weeks after the accident, but in August a bad fall at Salisbury brought home to him the fact that he was only one accident away from life in a wheelchair. His sight in one eye never returned entirely to normal.

Frankie suggested Ray should retire from riding and

4

become his agent. He was not unhappy with the job Andrew Stringer had done for him, but his strongest loyalty now lay with Ray, and the two men had formed a close bond since that fateful day in June. Ray accepted, and his shrewd knowledge and wise head have been greatly valued by Frankie ever since.

'Miraculous' has become a clichéd word in a sporting context, but its use is definitely appropriate when describing Frankie and Ray's escape that day. The day was a tragic one nonetheless, as it brought the death of Patrick, a close friend of the two, who left behind a wife, Gill. Exactly a week after the crash, Frankie and Ray attended Patrick's funeral. Despite neither being in a particularly fit state to travel, they were both keen to pay their respects to their friend, a man whose quick thinking had saved both their lives, but sadly was not enough to spare his own.

As he lay in agonising pain in his hospital bed, Frankie briefly considered giving up racing. He had a loving wife and a young son and didn't see any reason to continue. Fortunately for him, and the racing public who hold him in such affection, he soon snapped out of this negative mindset. Frankie Dettori's second life had begun.

CHAPTER 2

In Gianfranco's Shadow

Lanfranco Dettori was born in Milan, Italy, on 15 December 1970, with racing in his blood. His father Gianfranco was a 13 times Italian Champion Jockey, and he had three uncles who were also involved in racing, most notably Sergio, who had more than 1,500 winners.

But despite his father being an up-and-coming jockey at the time of his birth, Frankie was born into unhappy surroundings. His parents' marriage was on the rocks and this was to cause significant problems during his formative years.

His parents married after a whirlwind romance when his father visited a travelling circus next to the racecourse where he had been riding earlier that day in Milan. He was immediately mesmerised by a gorgeous young girl with long black hair who was part of the circus entourage. She had a variety of roles that evening, ranging from trapeze artist to juggler. Her masterpiece was being tied to a wheel of fortune whilst a bloke threw knives at her. Her name was Iris Maria, but everyone called her Mara.

Gianfranco made sure he met Mara later that night. It turned out she was only sixteen years old and had spent her entire life travelling with the circus, which originated in Russia. The courting period was brief, and they married after a few short months in 1963. However, it was not long before tensions arose.

Mara had only ever known life on the road and had hardly ever attended school because the circus was constantly moving. To this day she can hardly read or write. She only knew the nomadic life, and after her wedding she found it difficult to adapt to life as a jockey's wife.

Their first child, named Alessandra but known as Sandra, was born in 1965. Lanfranco (Frankie) followed five years later. The previous August, his father had met a woman called Christine whilst riding in Deauville. During that winter, which he'd spent riding in Australia, they had become close. It became increasingly important to Gianfranco to share his life with someone who had a similar passion for horses. Mara, for all her good points, hated horseracing and never really appreciated her husband's achievements. She loved him for the person he was, rather than for his professional achievements, which were completely lost on her. Instead, she preferred to retain her simple lifestyle – it was what she was used to and all she ever really understood.

After their parents separated, Frankie and Sandra stayed with their mother in Milan. Their father and Christine lived less than half a mile away but they saw very little of them when they were young because he was so busy as a jockey. This all changed when Frankie was five and his parents had a summit – Mara made it clear that she felt Gianfranco was in a much better position to give the children a decent start in life than she was, and that they should live mainly with him and Christine. At the same time she was quick to reassure the children she would always be there for them if they needed her.

The change in living arrangements was difficult for all parties. For Christine, it was a case of having to take on two of someone else's children who were very difficult and unfriendly. For Sandra the change was very distressing. She was eleven by this time and found it difficult to adapt to the new circumstances.

Christine believed the children should have a strict, traditional regime for the children, and was quick to lay down the law. If she instructed them to do something, it was to be obeyed without question. In many ways it resembled 1950s National Service – there was a strict timetable for going to bed, getting up, taking a bath and even brushing your teeth.

The children had a break at the weekends when they stayed with Mara, who took a far more laid back approach. She settled down with a man named Salvatore, and they are still together today. He took easily to the two children and always treated them as his own. Mara was very settled in her ways, and didn't miss being married to a multiple champion jockey one bit. She was far more suited to a simple life – looking after the laid-back, easy going Salvatore and working as a cleaner in Milan.

Living with this arrangement proved difficult for the young Frankie in many respects. Whilst his father's stature in Italy rocketed during the 1970s and saw him gain increasing notoriety abroad, to Frankie he seemed a very distant, cold figure. For example, during the summer he would only normally see his father one day a week. Gianfranco left home before he was up, and returned long after he'd gone to bed.

On rare days off Gianfranco seemed an intimidating, grim figure around the house in Frankie's young eyes. He would greet Frankie with a smile and a kiss, but this would be followed by long periods of silence as he watched the news on television, then retreated behind his newspaper for the rest of the evening to study the form for the following day. His riding always came first and Frankie wasn't encouraged to distract him.

Gianfranco was very much the strict disciplinarian around the house, in much the same mould as Christine. If Frankie stepped out of line, Sandra would often try to protect him. Gianfranco was also prone to harsh forms of punishment towards his two children. One such instance saw him make Sandra kneel in a tray of salt after she covered for Frankie.

Gianfranco was simply mirroring his own upbringing. He knew no other way. Nobody had ever shown him how to be a father. Today his relationship with his son is far more harmonious, he has become a far mellower character and they have formed a close bond, but back then this sort of relationship would have been unimaginable.

Winters meant Gianfranco leaving the family home to earn his living, and Frankie staying with his Godmother, Teresa Colangeli, who still is a trainer in Varese, having learnt the trade from her late husband Vincenzo. She played a memorable part in Frankie's upbringing and he has always maintained a close relationship with her, never forgetting the support and refuge she gave him as a child.

At the age of fourteen, life with Gianfranco and Christine had become too much for Sandra. She had told Frankie of her plans to escape back to Mara's house and one day she didn't return home from school. Predictably, Gianfranco reacted with fury and there was an enormous row. Frankie faced the reality of being left at home with his father and stepmother without the protection of his sister. However, the departure of Sandra forced Gianfranco to see that he had lost his daughter and he could be about to lose his son, too.

The very next day, Gianfranco went to collect his son from school for the first time ever, and happened to be driving a horsebox. Frankie was completely taken aback by this, and immediately ran up to the horsebox and leapt into the front seat next to his father, greeting him with a kiss.

Gianfranco told his son he was in for a big surprise. But what could this mean? Frankie's mind began to race as he attempted to contemplate what his father could be doing. They drove a few miles through Milan until they reached a field that contained three ponies, two that were bay and a palomino. Gianfranco told his son to pick one. Frankie, without hesitation, chose the palomino, prompted by its white face, mane and tail. For Frankie, this was love at first sight.

They took the pony home and put her in a field with stabling belonging to a neighbouring farmer.

Until now, Frankie's boyhood ambitions had nothing to do with racing. At first, he wanted to be a petrol pump attendant, and when he got a bit older he set his heart on being a professional footballer. But, on this day, when his father bought him Silvia the pony, Frankie finally inherited his father's passion for racing. He quickly formed a close bond with Silvia, and would show off in front of his friends from school as he rode her, pretending to be a jockey.

Gianfranco was keen to show his son early on that owning a pony came with responsibilities. On a rare day off, he took Frankie out to the stables and demonstrated how to groom her properly, telling him that he would only show him once. He began by brushing her coat, mane and tail; he then used a pitchfork to remove the dung in the box and replaced it with fresh straw; and he provided her with hay to eat and water to drink. Frankie watched on, being sure to take it all in. This was to prove a valuable lesson later on when he became an apprentice.

At first, Frankie found this new daily routine fun, and although, as the dark, cold winter mornings set in, it became a miserable chore, he always loved rushing home from school, donning the colours of Carlo d'Alessio and setting off on Silvia round the field.

Soon after his ninth birthday, Frankie put his hours of practice on Silvia to the test when he rode in his first Derby at the San Siro track in Milan. It was to be a baptism of fire. Silvia was by far the smallest pony in the race. The race started badly and got worse. Silvia became distracted by the crows at the finishing line and sent the young Frankie sprawling into a water jump.

But this humiliating setback wasn't nearly enough to put Frankie off riding. He had caught the bug and his heart was set on a career as a jockey. School became a bore for him and he spent each day dreaming of home time so he could get on Silvia and ride her around the field at high speed. There was, however, to be a major psychological obstacle for Frankie to overcome about a year later.

Silvia was, by now, a stubborn animal and increasingly difficult for Frankie to control. There were even days when he was too frightened to ride her. Then, one afternoon, she ran off with Frankie under a metal paddock rail. He grabbed the pole in a futile attempt to save himself, but it broke off in his hands, sending him crashing to the floor in excruciating pain, and leaving him needing hospital treatment. His father sold Silvia shortly afterwards. After this, Frankie temporarily fell out of love with riding – he didn't go near a horse for a whole year!

During this time Frankie flirted with his former passion of becoming a professional footballer, although this came to an abrupt end as his friends started to tower above him, making Frankie an easy target for some rough justice on the football pitch.

Frankie's passion for riding was rekindled when he began writing reports for the school magazine on the racing in Milan, usually dominated by flattering praise for his father's achievements. Frankie would spend hours cutting out pictures of his father in action and writing articles around them.

By now Frankie's relationship with his father had grown somewhat warmer and every once in a while Gianfranco would take his son with him to Rome at the weekend to watch him race. One day Gianfranco pointed out Lester Piggott, who had already won nine Derby winners, and told his son, 'You could be just as successful if you work hard enough.' This had a profound effect on Frankie. His enthusiasm was well and truly back. Within no time he was back at riding school for lessons. Before he knew it he was riding out in the school holidays with Carlo d'Alessio's string of horses. This usually meant taking the horses walking or trotting on the roads. If the horse was due for anything more rigorous he'd be replaced by a professional work rider.

One day, whilst walking the Milan course with his father, Frankie was amazed by the sight of a helicopter flying overhead and landing close by – something unheard of at Italian race meetings before then. Moments after the helicopter landed, the pale figure of Lester Piggott emerged, followed by trainer John Dunlop and other associates of Sheikh Mohammed, a member of the Royal family in Dubai who was in the process of expanding his racing interests. Gianfranco explained to his son that the Sheikh owned the filly Awaasif, who'd been sent from Britain to run in the Premio Del Jockey Club (a race she later won comfortably). Little did Frankie know it would only be a few short years before he would find himself working for the Sheikh.

At the age of thirteen and a half, Frankie's commitment to racing was unwavering and his father allowed him to leave school. The time had come for Frankie to take his first, tentative steps into the real world and make his living from racing.

His father sat him down and explained to him in no uncertain terms that the years ahead would test his resolve to the limit. He made it clear that for every small boy who set out to become a jockey only one in every thousand made it. Gianfranco had doubts in the back of his mind as to whether his son had the necessary aggression and motivation to make it, a suspicion fuelled by Frankie's humility in front of him, although this was due to the fact he felt intimidated by him.

Frankie set off to work full-time for Carlo d'Alessio and his trainers, Aldunio and Giuseppe Botti, for just £10 per week. Gianfranco was a stable jockey there and was held in high esteem by all who worked there. Inevitably, this meant that everyone there was afraid of giving the young Frankie any worthwhile challenges or treating him harshly. This was not helped by the reality that Frankie, weighing under five stone, was unable to ride big thoroughbreds. Also, although the forty racehorses owned by Carlo d'Alessio were among the classiest in Italy, Frankie was too young to be trusted to ride them, which inevitably meant he was stuck riding the slowest and quietest horses in the yard.

After the misery of school, Frankie initially enjoyed the new routine of caring for three horses at the stables. Each day he would discerningly brush their coats and do all the other menial tasks that were expected of him. But despite Frankie's efforts, his father was never satisfied when he turned up. His criticisms were relentless. This did not go unnoticed by the other workers and resulted in no one having much confidence in Frankie's ability.

Frankie's day did not stop once his shift had finished. At home, his father set a long pair of leather reins onto the metal frame of a well in the garden. This became the basis of nightly lessons from father to son, teaching him everything, from how to hold the reins to how to change his hands on the reins whilst holding a whip. Frankie was made to do this for half an hour or so each evening whilst his father sat and read a newspaper, occasionally glancing up to shout either criticism or support at his son.

This thorough and relentless teaching of the basics by Gianfranco was to hold his son in good stead for his career, and to this day Frankie can switch his whip or change his hands without effort, which gives him an enormous advantage over his rivals.

As winter approached, Gianfranco thought about sending Frankie to an indoor school until spring, but he feared he'd learn nothing but bad habits there. He decided his son was to be sent to his friend, the trainer Tonino Verdicchio's stables in the warmer climes of Pisa, three hours' drive away from Milan. Shortly before his fourteenth birthday in December 1984, Frankie began a journey that would prove the making of him.

Gianfranco gave Tonino precise instructions on how to treat Frankie: make him work hard and pay him peanuts. Tonino dutifully obliged. Tonino greeted Frankie warmly at the station in Pisa and took him home for a quick change. Straight away Frankie was put to work at his stables beside the local racecourse. Tonino armed Frankie with a pitchfork and a wheelbarrow, and ordered him to make a start on the twenty or so stables lined out in front of him – quite a jump from having just three to attend to in Milan.

Frankie did the job properly, as Sergio Cumani and Aldo Botti had shown him in the Milan stables. But things were different here and it wasn't long before Tonino made his displeasure clear. This place was run on a tight budget and Frankie's 'wasting' of straw didn't go down well. The rule here was to throw out the worst and put the rest back.

The lodging arrangements also came as a shock to Frankie – there was no spare bedroom, Frankie was to spend the next four months sleeping on the sofa. He found himself living with a large family – Tonino was married to Antonietta and they had three daughters. Yet despite the strict work regime, domestic life was always very happy and he was treated as one of the family.

Frankie found riding Tonino's horses a steep learning curb. He regularly struggled to control the big, hard-pulling horses. Falls were frequent, and bumps and bruises were aplenty. But by now nobody could doubt Frankie's hunger and determination and he always got straight back in the saddle after a fall. Tonino was a hard taskmaster, but he mixed this with good humour. Although this was a tough four months for Frankie, they were also very happy times. It was his first experience of normal, family life, and was also the time when he began to come out of his shell – thanks largely to the rapport he built up with Tonino's girls.

His stay ended the following March, just as his father completed a riding tour of Australia and South Africa. Gianfranco collected his son from Pisa and on the journey back to Milan started to outline his grand plan for his son's future. He wanted Frankie to spend six months in Britain, followed by six months in France, after which he'd let him come home to Italy for the following summer. He'd clearly thought carefully about this, realising that in those days apprentices in Italy could start riding in races when they were fifteen and a half. He had timed Frankie's homecoming to the dot.

At first Frankie wasn't keen on the idea. Travelling to Britain, in particular, seemed daunting to him. He'd been useless at English at school, and besides, he was only just starting to come out of his shell. Predictably, his father's will was to prevail, but not before Frankie had had the chance to impress, and then frighten his father.

Upon arriving back in Milan, Frankie demonstrated to his father how much he had learnt whilst in Pisa. Gianfranco was visibly shocked by what he saw, and within days Frankie was working with top-class horses due to run in the Italian Classics. For the first time Gianfranco was truly proud of his son, further fuelling his ambition for Frankie. The medium-term future was mapped out. Frankie was to travel to Britain to join Luca Cumani, son of Sergio. But there was soon to be one major setback that would put the dreams of Frankie, and indeed Gianfranco, in grave danger.

By now Frankie was travelling to work at the yard on a moped. He would always time the mile-long journey and make it his mission to beat his record each day. He considered himself too cool to wear a crash helmet and would even resort to skipping red lights in pursuit of a faster time.

One morning as he approached a junction leading to the stables, on track to break his personal best, he pushed his luck a step too far. The road forked into two – one way was for cars and bikes, the other was for horses and had sand on top of the tarmac. Frankie chose the latter, causing his moped to skid, and sending him hurtling along the ground before careering into a large lamppost. His head hurt at the time but it was his right elbow that was to be of most serious concern.

He was swiftly taken to hospital by ambulance and X-rays confirmed he'd shattered his elbow into over twenty pieces. His father was enraged with his son for such reckless behaviour, and he and Christine didn't let the fact they were in a hospital stop them from giving him a massive verbal dressing down.

That said, Gianfranco swiftly arranged for his son to be moved to a private hospital, and he was operated on soon after. A few days later Gianfranco was riding a horse called Wild Dancer in the Italian 2,000 Guineas. He was denied victory by the narrowest of margins by a certain Irish jockey called Michael Kinane riding Again Tomorrow. There was no doubt that Frankie's career-threatening injuries proved an unwelcome distraction to Gianfranco's preparations for the race.

Recovery from this setback was painfully slow, and Frankie initially found he could not extend his elbow 45 degrees. This improved very gradually with the aid of daily physiotherapy. But after eleven weeks, his father's patience with the medical profession ran out.

Gianfranco took his son to Aldo Botti's yard and loaded him on board a horse called Fire Thatch who had formerly been trained by Henry Cecil in Britain. Frankie knew his arm was still far from repaired but his father didn't allow any time for discussion. It turned out this horse was called Fire Thatch with good reason.

In a split second, Fire Thatch set off at lightning pace. In one moment of extreme pain, Frankie found both arms straight out in front of him, something there was no way he could have managed a few seconds previously. One minute later he'd covered five furlongs and the elbow damage was largely cured. To this day he cannot stretch out his right arm as much he should be able to, but there was no career-threatening damage after this rather unconventional cure.

As soon as his recovery was complete, Gianfranco was keen to send him to Britain as quickly as possible. Frankie had already been introduced to Luca Cumani at an Italian race meeting. Luca had been a superb amateur rider, later becoming Henry Cecil's assistant, before setting up on his own as a trainer at Newmarket.

On 10 July 1985, Frankie flew from Milan with one million lira in his pocket (£366) and an identification tag around his neck. Upon arrival at Luton, he was met by Luca's chauffeur David, who tried to make Frankie feel welcome despite not being able to speak a word of Italian. But Frankie was about to experience a positive omen. On the journey from the airport they listened to the July race meeting at Newmarket on the radio. Frankie heard the name of a horse called Lanfranco being called in the commentary of the big race of the day. Home wasn't so far away after all.

CHAPTER 3

Harsh Lessons In Newmarket

Arriving in Britain as a fourteen year old boy was naturally a culture shock for Frankie. For the first few months, he was an introvert, the exact opposite of the motor mouth we know him as today. Homesickness was to prove a major obstacle he would be forced to overcome. He found fitting in and making friends extremely difficult. He spoke little English, and faced many difficulties adapting to the cultural differences.

Upon arriving in Newmarket he headed for the house in Bury Road where he was to live for the first few weeks. Luca Cumani's chauffeur, David, suggested Frankie leave his belongings outside the front door, convinced it would be relatively safe. Frankie was reluctant to do this as if he had done this in Milan the bag would almost certainly be gone when he returned.

He was taken by David straight to Luca Cumani's

yard, and his secretary took him to the bottom yard where he met Arthur Taylor. Frankie took some comfort from the fact this man could speak some Italian because he had fought there in the war as a sergeant in the Cavalry regiment, and, as he found out much later, had been involved in the battle for Montecassino at the same time as his grandfather.

Frankie was still in his suit, but Arthur handed him a dandy brush and a towel so he could start dressing the filly and he got straight down to work. Luca put in an appearance half an hour later and after a brief introduction told Frankie to be in the yard by six the next morning.

Frankie returned to the house to find his bag was still there, much to his surprise. The whole family was there to greet him, and he was shown to his room, which turned out to be more of a cell than a bedroom, containing a small bed, a sink and a cupboard. Beside the basin was a jug of orange squash. Frankie poured himself a glass and took a sip, then spat it straight out again. He'd only been used to freshly-squeezed orange juice in Italy and had no idea you had to dilute orange squash with water.

Things got no better when he sat down for his first evening meal. His hosts gave him ravioli out of a Heinz tin to try to make him feel at home. As his meal was placed in front of him he was struck by the smell, which for him seemed nauseating and not at all like the ravioli he was used to eating at home. He tried a spoonful out of politeness but found it unbearable. And conversation was impossible because he didn't speak any English. He only understood one word that came from the mouth of his new landlord, Swinburn. It turned out the landlord was a huge fan of trainer Michael Stoute and tried to make Frankie feel more familiar with him by constantly talking about Stoute and Swinburn's achievements, often talking about Shergar in particular.

When Frankie arrived at Luca's yard the next morning he was totally overwhelmed by the size of it and the number of horses he could see on Newmarket heath, and with good reason. At the time, there were around sixty trainers based there, and Luca alone had over one hundred horses to his name.

It was quickly made clear what was expected of Frankie. Despite the language barrier, he swiftly realised that most of the people who worked there were in awe of Luca. He had a strict regime and expected everything to be done properly, without cutting corners.

As a fourteen-year-old lad, in a foreign country, unable to speak a word of the language, Frankie was understandably introverted upon his arrival and found it difficult to make friends. Furthermore, few of the lads made much effort to get to know him, with one exception, a much older man called George Dunwoody, father of Richard Dunwoody. Frankie was instantly struck by George's kindness and willingness to make time for him. Most mornings they would have breakfast together sitting on the straw.

But George was the exception. Many of the stable lads picked on the young Frankie, mocking his voice and getting him to do all the dirty jobs around the yard. Frankie responded by being especially discerning about his job –arriving first thing in the morning long before the other lads, and taking meticulous care over each and every horse he was responsible for. For the first six months he would either be working or sleeping, he had made no real friends and was eager to impress Luca with his enthusiasm.

This was buoyed up by weekly phone calls from his father. Gianfranco would remind his son that this groundwork was essential if he wanted to fly in private planes, and own big cars, and generally live the lifestyle of his heroes such as Pat Eddery and Lester Piggott one day. It was this encouragement and the reminder of what could come about from the seemingly thankless work if he remained truly dedicated and disciplined that kept the young Frankie going. But he was lonely and still missed the Italian lifestyle and his old friends, and as a result would regularly cry himself to sleep at night.

Life got somewhat easier for Frankie after he formed a friendship with Valfredo Valiani, another Italian apprentice at the yard, who would eventually have success as a trainer winning the 2001 Yorkshire Oaks with the filly Super Tassa. Things got better still when his English started to improve and he formed firm friendships with Colin Rate and Andy Keates, with whom he had previously fought. But Frankie's rapidly improving English actually didn't help much when it came to speaking to Colin, who had a strong Sunderland accent, which even most English people would struggle with. To this day, however, they remain best friends and speak on a daily basis.

Andy comes from a racing family. His uncle, Joe Mercer, had been champion jockey in 1979 and another of his uncles, Manny Mercer, was tragically killed in a fall at Ascot. Despite earning a few rides for Luca, he didn't make it as a jockey and became Frankie's driver and faithful servant, as he remains to this day.

Overtime Frankie was becoming increasingly like his old, extroverted self, and began to come out of his shell more and more as these friendships developed. Inevitably, Colin and Andy began to lead the young Frankie astray, and got him into the habit of spending afternoons in betting shops. A typical day around this time involved lunch at the New Astley Club after the morning's work, followed by snooker and pool, then across the road to Cuthie Suttle's betting shop where they'd spend the afternoon.

But this firm bond didn't excuse Frankie from the initiation ceremony given to all newcomers. One morning, after work, and completely without warning, a gang of stable lads held Frankie down near the dung heap, removed his pants and encouraged one of the girls to cover his private parts with hoof oil, then they shafted a carrot up his backside and left him wriggling on the floor to the sound of loud applause. Removing the carrot was easy enough but it took many days of scrubbing before the grease and oil were gone.

The only serious problem Frankie had by this stage was his lodgings. He hated being stuck in such a small room and was constantly irritated by the five children.

On Sundays he was expected to take his own washing to the launderette and feed himself. This usually meant going for a large Wimpy whilst his clothes were drying. He was paying too much money for not much comfort and was keen to move on. A stable lad called David Sykes told Frankie of a spare room at his parent's council house. He took Frankie to meet them and they were willing to let him move in immediately. Home life with Val and Dennis Sykes felt much better and was the final part of the jigsaw that made Frankie feel comfortable in his new country.

Living with this couple was in stark contrast to life at home with his father. He was free to stay out late with Colin and Andy at weekends. Frankie was far too young to go to pubs legally, but he managed to smuggle himself in by smearing newspaper print on his face to make him look older.

Now that he was fully comfortable with life in Britain, the outgoing, cheeky Frankie we know today started to surface. The perfectionist when working in the stables was replaced by a rebellious rascal who would frequently get on the wrong side of Luca. He began ducking work as much as possible and did the one thing you don't do to Luca – cut corners.

Frankie also began standing up for himself as his confidence grew. When the older, bigger lads picked on him he would respond by flooding the box he was working in, which would take a long time to clear up.

He and Colin were the lightest apprentices on Luca's books, so they would be given the job of braking in young horses bought by him, to get them used to having a saddle and jockey on their backs. For fun, they would race these young horses against each other, with Frankie pretending to be Steve Cauthen and Colin mimicking Pat Eddery. They used branches from a hedge as whips and raced at ferocious speed as their rivalry grew more intense by the day.

Forcing youngsters to run faster than they should is reckless and they would often end up covered in sweat, gasping for breath. Inevitably, they were eventually caught by the stud's head lad, who immediately grassed them up to Luca. Unsurprisingly, Luca was bursting with rage and gave them the bollocking of a lifetime in his office. They were threatened with all sorts of punishments if they did it again, including what Frankie considered to be the ultimate punishment – being transferred to Midlands trainer Reg Hollinshead, who had a reputation that made Luca seem a pussycat.

By now Frankie's English had improved greatly, he had a good social life, and wasted hours in pubs, discos and snooker halls. He was enjoying his new life and was somewhat reluctant to return home to Italy for the Christmas holiday, unsure whether his father would send him back to Newmarket.

Fortunately for Frankie he was to return there in January, where he experienced a long, bleak winter. Conditions were so bad that all racing came to a halt for most of February and early March. Working in the stables in those conditions was not easy. It was impossible to keep warm no matter how many layers of clothing he wore, but the daily chores and Luca's stringent regime carried on as normal.

Of course, afternoons were still spent in Cuthie Suttle's betting shop. With the absence of racing, Frankie turned his attention to the greyhounds and became quite an expert. Sneakily, he'd always bet on traps 1 or 6, and tried to delay handing over his slip until he'd seen if his selection had jumped well out of the traps.

Frankie was a shrewd gambler (most of the time) and had learnt to take advantage of tips he could gather through people he knew. Prior to the Christmas break, George Dunwoody confided in Frankie that his son Richard would win the Grand National on West Tip. The horse had fallen at Becher's Brook on the second circuit the previous year. Frankie put his last £5 on West Tip at 33-1 that lunchtime and topped it up a few weeks later with another £5 at 28-1. As the winter progressed, George became more and more confident that Richard would win and was quick to pass this on to Frankie. Week on week Frankie would put an extra £5 or £10 on the horse to win, skilfully negotiating the price with Cuthie, which was shortening rapidly. By the time the big day arrived, West Tip was the favourite at 15-2.

Frankie watched the race at home with Val and Dennis, his eyes fixated anxiously at the unfolding drama as he sat on the edge of the arm of the sofa. The horse showed ice coolness throughout the race, while Richard Dunwoody rode with the conviction and experience of a man far beyond his years. Richard wisely waited until he had jumped the last fence before accelerating towards the finish, securing a convincing victory.

Frankie leaped out of his seat and ran out of the house to collect his winnings. He was on cloud nine – he normally only had a spare £20 at the end of the week, but this win was worth about £1,900 due to George's tip-off.

He repaid the kindness shown to him by his hosts by buying Val a much-needed new washing machine and iron. On the Monday he treated himself to a decent Vespa scooter, which would soon expose the wilder elements of his personality and lead him into trouble with the law.

The first inkling of the problems to come came not long after Frankie bought the Vespa, when two policemen turned up on Val's doorstep. Frankie had been caught riding on pavements, but Val managed to bail him out by telling the policemen he couldn't speak or read a word of English. Somehow it worked!

By this time he had become such a regular at Cuthie's betting shop that he started working there when money was tight, being paid £5 to work the afternoon shift, which generally involved writing the latest prices on the wall in the final moments of trading or writing out the results. Cuthie overlooked the practical problems with this arrangement, such as the fact Frankie was too short to reach the top of the board or that his spelling was terrible as nobody seemed to mind and the meagre wages he was paid generally ended up back in Cuthie's hands, such was Frankie's obsession with gambling. This obsession would lead to Frankie's most serious dispute with Luca thus far.

Frankie and most of the other stable lads had lost

money on a horse called Saker at York one afternoon in May 1986. He had always impressed at the yard and seemed destined for greatness, but never really performed when put to the test at a higher level.

That evening, a furious Frankie went round the yard and told anyone who would listen that Luca couldn't train a bicycle. He stupidly repeated this to the second head lad, Stuart Jackson. When Luca put in an appearance later, Stuart asked him what the Italian word for bicycle was. Luca asked him why he wanted to know, then Stuart dropped him right in it by repeating Frankie's harsh comments. The look on Luca's face left Frankie in no doubt he was in huge trouble.

Luca grabbed Frankie by the collar, lifted him into the air and threw him against the wall. He delivered a firm warning, while shaking him alike an alarm clock, shouting ferociously in Italian: 'Maybe I can't train a bicycle Frankie, but while you work for me I will always be the greatest trainer in the world. Do you understand?'

The impact of the bollocking soon wore off and the following afternoon Frankie was back in the betting shop trying to recoup his losses. Nobody can doubt that his gambling was irresponsible – he was too young to even be on the premises and really it shouldn't have been encouraged – but a series of lucky coincidences happened there and he met people through it who would go on to have a profound impact upon his life.

One such person was Peter Burrell, who was constantly looking for new challenges. Within days of meeting, Pete had agreed to look after Frankie's business affairs. Pete was new to the management game, and found the challenge daunting in those early days, and both of them learnt how it was done as they went along. This led to a firm trust between them that has always remained in tact. Frankie wouldn't have it any other way and has resisted all offers to sign up with multi-million pound agencies who are only interested in exploiting him as a brand and are not interested in what's best for him as a person.

He knows that Pete genuinely has his best interests at heart and will not take him for a ride. All decisions are made jointly and they speak at least twice a day. Even with Frankie's success, Pete has kept his ambitions modest, only taking on a small portfolio of clients he knows he can serve well, all of whom are close friends of Frankie's. Aside from Frankie, his 'Classic Management' portfolio consists of former footballer turned actor Vinnie Jones, chef Marco Pierre White, who is now working at Frankie's restaurants, former boxer Barry McGuigan and up-and-coming food writer Alex Antonioni.

Another character Frankie met through the betting shop was Mattie Cowing, who bore an uncanny resemblance to the comedian Mike Reid with his gruff voice and earthy sense of humour. Mattie had been a factory worker making boxes until a stroke prevented him from continuing, but did allow him to indulge in his passion for racing. At first, Mattie regarded Frankie as a mad Italian rascal who was going nowhere and turned him down when he first asked him to book his rides. But Frankie persisted and they became firm friends, with Frankie even paying for a much needed heart bypass for Mattie some years later, which gave him an extra five years of health and happiness with his wife before passing away.

What, at the time, seemed like wasted afternoons throwing money away in a rundown betting shop have proved a blessing in disguise. The pocket money he wasted was made up for in the friends he made on those cold winter afternoons.

CHAPTER 4

Ready for the Off

By the summer of 1986 Frankie was anxious to get his riding career underway and put the skills he'd been practising over the last few years to the test. Regulations meant that he couldn't ride in Britain until his sixteenth birthday, but in Italy he could start at fifteen and a half. His father set up three rides a week for him towards the end of June, so Frankie promptly set off for Milan, where he met with the local stewards and was granted a licence.

Frankie made his riding debut at Milan racecourse on a filly called My Charlotte on Wednesday, 25 June. This was not to be a day to remember. Nerves probably got the better of Frankie – he had been building up to and dreaming of this day for years, but the horse got off to a poor start and never recovered, leaving him trailing in last place.

A tough lecture from Gianfranco followed, and three days later Frankie was back in the saddle, this time on a large chestnut filly trained by Aldunio Botti called Maria di Scozia. This was to be a tough test over nine furlongs for the young Frankie, not least because he would be up against no fewer than three members of his own family in this race – his father, his uncle Sergio and his cousin Robert.

Things started well, and he quickly gained a slender lead. Coming into the bend he was still in front and on the straight things were looking good. Frankie began to hear screaming coming from behind him, which seemed to be getting gradually louder. It was none other than his father ordering his son and protégé to move over to the rail. This was followed by more instructions to hit her and to keep pushing. With two furlongs to go, Frankie and Maria di Scozia were exhausted. Two horses quickly passed, one of them, Gianfranco on Nina Hagen, sprinting by with less than a hundred yards to go. Frankie managed to hang on for third, leaving him feeling generally proud of his day's work. As he made his way back to the unsaddling enclosure, the crowd started jeering and making gestures at Frankie, leaving him bewildered and embarrassed. He had no idea at this stage why he had received such a negative reaction from the crowd who treated him as something of a laughing stock.

A stewards' inquiry was called. Frankie watched a replay of the race next to his father in the stewards' room. Things quickly became clear. It turned out the reason for the hysteria was because Gianfranco could be seen blatantly beating the backside of Frankie's horse with his own whip on the bend. Suspicions were raised due to the fact the two horses came from the same ownership and could have been coupled together for betting purposes – in other words, allowing punters to pick up their winnings if either horse won. They probably got off with a lecture because Frankie didn't win, but if he had hung on in the straight his career, along with that of his father, could have been seriously jeopardised, if not ended there and then.

After gaining third place on his final ride of the week in Turin, Frankie headed back to Newmarket, where he would experience the sweet taste of success for the first time soon after, riding the winner at the annual Donkey Derby at the Recreation Fields at Newmarket, seeing off far more experienced riders in the process who struggled to adapt to the stubborn, unpredictable nature of donkeys.

In the final, Frankie gave a masterful salute as he crossed the winning post. Finally he had won something. It was a small-scale event, but at last, there were signs things were really starting to come together.

His first real win would come that November in Turin. Gianfranco had always planned for his son's return to Italy in early November but Luca Cumani had reservations. Up-and-coming jockeys can claim a weight allowance until they have won a certain number of winners, and Luca did not want that allowance used up riding in low profile races in Italy. In the end, Gianfranco's wish prevailed, and the scene was set on 16 November for Frankie to take Turin racecourse by storm, albeit on a grey day in front of a handful of hardcore punters.

Gianfranco had bought his son a horse called Rif to develop his skills on, a tough horse that liked bottomless ground. This freezing, wet, miserable day would be perfect conditions for Rif, and Frankie had overcome his nerves of earlier that year.

They started well and pulled out into the straight, Frankie winning without ever really needing to test his skills. He was overcome with emotion and naturally wanted to let off steam, but with his father standing nearby, and with his upbringing, he had to keep his feet firmly on the ground.

Further success followed the next day when Frankie took part in an apprentice race at Livorno, during which he teamed up with the young trainer Andrea Picorarro, who had been working for Luca at Newmarket.

Frankie spent that winter in Naples working in a satellite yard run for Aldo Botti by his assistant Peo Perlante. Frankie spent many hours in the public sauna to shed the pounds, where he got to know the experienced jockey Bruce Raymond. They built a strong rapport and to this day Frankie regularly turns to him for advice and support, taking solace from Bruce's old-fashioned, gentlemanly manner.

He lived on a council estate in the home of one of the yard men, Tonino Cantante. In Naples, Frankie found himself surrounded by other, more established apprentices, and gaining regular rides proved hard. This situation was not helped by Peo Perlante, who would only give Frankie rides if there was no one else available, which could perhaps be put down to an old rift with Gianfranco.

This left Frankie in the perilous position of having to rely on other stables for spare rides. He spent that winter gaining valuable experience on low-key races away from the limelight, tallying fifteen winners over four months. Luca kept a regular eye on Frankie's progress, unhappy at the fact that he was wasting his claiming allowance on such low-profile races. The moment Frankie won his fifteenth winner in Naples, the 7 pound claiming allowance granted to apprentices in Britain had been used up.

Luca made contact with Gianfranco where he made it clear it was essential Frankie returned to Newmarket, which he duly did the following spring. Momentously, Frankie's sixteenth birthday had now passed and his riding career in Britain was set to begin.

However, at first the opportunities for rides were limited and the flat racing season was well over a month old before he was booked to ride on 33-1 shot Mustakbil at Kempton's bank holiday meeting. Frankie was booked by Derby winning trainer Peter Walwyn, known as Basil for his resemblance to the John Cleese character in Fawlty Towers. Frankie entered the race 4 pounds overweight, and with his claiming allowance used up this did not endear him to his bosses.

The race began well, but the horse tired in the final furlong due to lack of fitness. After the race, Walwyn asked Frankie what went wrong, to which Frankie responded by pointing at the horse's tummy and replying, 'Not fit'. Walwyn, a champion trainer, was having none of it, and was incandescent with rage as he said, 'What! Not fit! You cheeky little bugger. Not fit!' Walwyn wasted little time in ringing Luca to tell him he wouldn't be hiring Frankie's services for another year.

Frankie's first win in Britain came in impressive style at Goodwood on 9 June, where he was riding Lizzy Hare, named after Luca's secretary, dismissed as a 12-1 shot. The horse was promising, but Frankie found himself pitted against three champion jockeys in the shape of Steve Cauthen, Pat Eddery and Willie Carson. It was Willie's horse, Betty Jane who did the early running until Steve took over on Interlacing.

Frankie then managed to squeeze his horse through the pack via a gap on the far rail, winning by a comfortable one and a half lengths. Frankie had won his first winner in immaculate style, beating three highly respected champion jockeys in the process including his great hero, Steve Cauthen.

In the weeks that followed he found himself riding at least twice a week, often being priced at long odds and never really standing a chance of winning. One of the highlights of that summer was riding Merle in the Royal Hunt Cup at Royal Ascot, giving Frankie his first taste of riding in front of a packed house.

His second win would eventually come at Ripon on 24 June, riding Crown Ridge. The following evening he was back riding Lizzy Hare at Goodwood and won again, making it two winners in two days, giving a much-needed boost to his self-esteem.

However, self-confidence would ultimately turn to

arrogance and unpleasant cockiness in July. Frankie rode Camallino Rose to victory, beating favourite Rae Guest on Luca's colt Fill My Glass at Carlisle. Although Frankie had only won on a photo finish, it proved enough to cause him to give Rae a verbal bashing on the way back to unsaddle, which was noticed by his fellow jockeys and Ivan Allen, owner of the winning horse.

The jockeys got their revenge on Frankie next time he rode Camallino Rose at Hamilton, in a four horse race which Frankie should have won comfortably. The jockeys managed to box Frankie in for the entire race in what turned out to be a successful attempt to teach him a lesson about bad sportsmanship.

That said, Frankie managed to land himself in serious trouble just two days later when he won an apprentice race on Local Hero, trained by Luca. Second in that race was Red River Boy, ridden by another of Luca's apprentices, Stephen Quane, who immediately objected to the stewards, claiming Frankie's horse had crossed in front of him. The stewards ruled in Frankie's favour, but Stephen's trainer Ron Hodges took things further by appealing against the Ascot stewards' decision, which resulted in a hearing at the Jockey Club's headquarters. Luca and the solicitor did enough to get the appeal thrown out. Frankie was off the hook.

His first experience of the high life came in August when he travelled to a meeting at Brighton with Steve Cauthen in his chauffeur-driven Jaguar. Steve had built up a considerable friendship with Frankie and had always taken time to speak to him. Going into the Brighton meeting, Steve needed just two more winners to reach the 1,000 mark in Britain. He took one of the early races, and was all set to reach the momentous landmark when Frankie threw a spanner in the works by narrowly beating Steve when his horse Know All beat Steve on In The Habit in a tight finish.

Luckily, all was forgiven and Frankie didn't end up walking home as Steve ended up with the final win he needed, cruising to victory on Picnicing in the last race of the day.

The rest of the season would prove far less fruitful for Frankie, a situation not helped when he was forced to move out of Val and Dennis' home after two happy years – the local council had discovered Frankie was living there, which meant Val and Dennis were in breach of council house regulations. He was reluctant to leave, but understood they could lose their home if he continued to reside there.

In what was meant to be a temporary, month-long arrangement, Frankie moved in with his friend Bernice Emanuel who agreed to put him up in her spare room. The month ended up being two and a half years.

There was to be one more winner for Frankie that summer, his eighth of the year, in a maiden race on Luca's filly, Sumara. The horse was owned by one Sheikh Mohammed. Neither could have dreamt of the influence they would eventually have on one another's racing careers as Frankie eased to a convincing victory that afternoon at Haydock.

Frankie assumed he would be spending the upcoming winter in Naples as he had done the previous year, but this time Luca asserted his authority, believing it to be a waste of time whilst also wasting his valuable claiming allowance. Instead, he held long talks with Gianfranco and they decided it would be better to send Frankie to California where he would be employed as a work rider for Richard Cross, one of Luca's former assistants, at Santa Anita racecourse.

He was to benefit from being in California during a vintage period during which a number of legendary jockeys were riding there, such as Fernando Toro, Laffit Pincay, Chris McCarron and Eddie Delahoussaye. One of Frankie's heroes, the late Bill Shoemaker, was in the twilight of his career by then but was still capable of putting in an impressive finish, and Frankie made the most of the opportunity to watch and learn from him.

Yet it was probably Angel Cordero from whom Frankie learnt the most during his time in California. Like Frankie, he was the charismatic showman of his generation, the crowd's favourite jockey. To Frankie, Angel was the perfect jockey. He was by now in his late forties but still able to make riding to the highest standards look easy. Frankie studied every last detail of Angel's technique and made no secret of his desire to imitate his style in a number of areas, such as the way he crouched very low on a horse's back to keep wind resistance to a minimum.

After the Breeders' Cup, Angel invited Luca and Frankie to dinner at his house in New York. This was to be one of the most important evenings of Frankie's young life.

He explained to Frankie the advantages of riding with just his toes in the stirrups, in sharp contrast to the usual European method of putting both feet firmly in the irons. This, he explained, gives the jockey more feeling and balance. Angel was by no means the only American jockey to ride in this way; there are numerous other examples, including Frankie's other great hero and friend, Steve Cauthen.

For once, Frankie sat in silence and took in everything Angel was saying. After dinner, Angel took him to his gym to give Frankie the chance to try out this technique on his mechanical horse. It was like going back to square one in many ways. Frankie felt as though he was putting a severe strain on the back of his calf muscles, but Angel persuaded him to persevere. It would be several years before Frankie would put this to the test.

He finally experimented with it in Hong Kong, riding out in the mornings when he thought nobody else was looking. As with his first attempt in Angel's gym, it was painful to begin with, causing sharp pains in the back of his calves. It wasn't long though before he started developing thicker muscles on his calves and extra lumps of muscle on top of his feet.

The change in stance also meant a change in balance. In America, where riding this way is commonplace, saddles are considerably further forward, and jockeys aren't pulling on their horse's mouths. Over time Frankie would try to combine the best of both worlds and come up with his own technique.

This meant he would start each race riding the European way in an attempt to keep the horse relaxed, before switching to the American stance in the second half, creating a neater finish whilst also restricting the impact wind resistance has when finishing a race. Nearly twenty years on, most jockeys riding in Britain have adapted to riding with their toes in the irons.

Frankie had always ridden with his right leg shorter in the stirrups than his left, an essential cardinal of this technique, known in America as 'acey-deucey' which gives riders a better balance on the American tracks, which are all left-handed.

There was, however, one further trait Frankie picked up from Angel during his first spell in California that would become an integral part of his make-up some nine years later. Angel was very much the extroverted showman of American racing, and would produce a flying dismount after winning races. Frankie began practising his flying dismount in the quiet of Richard Cross' yard in front of a small audience of bemused Mexican horsewalkers and grooms.

Another of that winter's valuable lessons that would stay with him for life was to learn to ride against the clock, something that is second nature to American jockeys. Frankie managed to perfect his gallop to within fractions of a second, allowing him to become a brilliant judge of pace and be confident in making the running in races.

He spent that first winter in America living with Richard's family at their home in Pasadena, a short ride from Santa Anita racecourse. The daily routine was more pleasant than at Newmarket and was altogether more scenic with the stunning backdrop the San Gabriel mountains provided. As with Newmarket, work began at dawn in the usual way, which would be followed by riding up to ten horses round the tight, left-hand track.

Once this was over Frankie had the rest of the day to himself, which typically involved playing cards in the track kitchen, often with Johnny Longden, the American jockey who was by then in his eighties, before watching the afternoon racing with a few fun bets to go with it. This is probably not the rigorous regime Luca expected when he sent Frankie to Richard Cross.

Another hobby Frankie developed was mimicking the techniques of the leading jockeys before inviting Richard's grooms to identify who he was impersonating, the three favourites being Angel Cordero, Bill Shoemaker and Chris McCarron.

Without realising it, Frankie was picking up the best from all these legendary American jockeys and developing it into his own unique style.

CHAPTER 5

Hard Lessons

Frankie began the 1988 season stronger and more confident than before, thanks to the skills he had developed and enhanced in California. Finding decent rides, however, was still a major problem as he was far from established.

At the end of April, Luca was struggling to find a rider for Heroes Sash in a valuable race at Haydock. Ray Cochrane, who was at Newmarket that day for the 2,000 Guineas, persuaded Luca to take a chance on Frankie. Heroes Sash didn't win, but Frankie did little wrong and this did not go unnoticed.

Things really began to take off in June: Frankie rode his first double on Norman Invader and Mischievous Miss at Redcar, and then shortly after he achieved success on Follow The Drum at Folkestone.

At this stage, though, Frankie was far from the

finished article and there were some high-profile examples of the recklessness of youth coming to the public's attention. Firstly, there was the race at Catterick in early July when Frankie won on one of Luca's horses, Casey. They should have won easily, but arrogance got the better of Frankie. He eased the horse heavily in the closing stages and came mighty close to losing the race when Kirsheda put in a sprint in the final stretch, causing a photo finish. Frankie had just held on.

On the way back to unsaddle, Frankie was hit by a tide of abuse from the punters and received a severe telling off from the stewards for being too confident. The following morning he was front page news in the Racing Post which led with the headline 'Frankie Lives Dangerously'. This wasn't to be the end of the matter.

A few days later Luca called Frankie into his office to watch the race with him on video before aiming another of his legendary bollockings in Frankie's direction. Even worse, a photograph of the finish arrived from Casey's owner Gerald Leigh. Attached was a note which read, 'Too much attention to the camera and not enough to the finish!'

More stupidity was to follow, on an altogether more serious level this time. Frankie had enjoyed success on Norman Invader in June, but within a few weeks the horse had almost killed Frankie's close friend Andy Keates in an accident at the yard. Andy suffered serious head injuries along with broken bones in his jaw and cheeks which kept him off work for weeks.

Frankie callously sought revenge on the horse for this incident and took his chance when he was booked to ride him in the Magnet Cup at York. Frankie had taped a piece of lead into the flap of his whip. As they moved into contention in the final three furlongs, Frankie started to hit the horse with his enhanced whip with overpowering malice.

His best friend Colin Rate was coming up on the inside on Chartino, but was affected by Norman Invader, who was responding to the aggressive whip action by hanging left handed, nearly causing Colin to go over the rails. It was miraculous for Frankie that the stewards didn't pick up on his actions in that race, but Luca was not so remiss and Frankie was in serious trouble. One small mercy was that Luca never did find out about the lead taped into the whip, which would almost certainly have been enough to cause Frankie to be sacked.

Ten days later events proved that even then Frankie hadn't learnt his lesson and that he was still prone to mistreating horses. He was booked to ride Torkabar, owned by the Aga Khan at Catterick. He was the clear favourite for the race but had let Frankie down in his previous ride at York and was prone to spurts of unpredictability.

The race started badly and Torkabar didn't react well to Frankie's attempts to get him going. They finished a hugely disappointing third. Frankie reacted badly to this, lashing his whip over the horse's head. It was done out of sheer frustration, but it was completely unacceptable nonetheless.

This time the stewards weren't so lenient, and duly banned Frankie for three days for improper riding. Of course, the real consequences were to come back at the yard. The following morning when he was standing in the doorway of a stable, with a pitchfork in his hand idly shuffling the straw, he was given an almighty boot up the backside courtesy of Ray Cochrane, followed by a raging lecture about how he'd let the whole stable down, especially since the horse was owned by the stable's principal owner, the Aga Khan.

More was to follow. Luca was away in America at the sales when the incident occurred but found out what had happened upon his return and suspended Frankie from riding for a further two weeks.

Luca was becoming increasingly concerned by Frankie's lack of discipline and erratic moments that led to catastrophic madness. It became semi-official policy for second head lad Stuart Jackson to give Frankie a kick in the backside whenever he was boasting of his achievements, or, really, whenever he felt like it.

Yet despite these alarming flaws, Frankie's natural talent was undeniable and he was gaining a reputation far beyond the confines of Luca's yard. That August, multiple champion trainer Henry Cecil turned to Frankie when Steve Cauthen was injured. Frankie felt humbled and flattered that he was being considered an adequate replacement for such a legendary figure as Steve.

Frankie's first success for him came at Newmarket on

Opening Verse, a horse that went on to win the Breeders' Cup in America. Frankie followed this win by a victory at Wolverhampton as part of another double. And even more exciting times lay ahead before the season drew to a close.

In late September he was called into Luca's office to be told that the Aga Khan would be running two pacemakers for the Derby winner Kahyasi in the Prix de l'Arc de Triomphe. It had been decided that Frankie would ride one of them, Roushayd.

When the big day arrived, things didn't exactly go to plan. It started as they'd intended, with Rae Guest towing the field for the first mile on Taboushkan. The plan was for Frankie to take over on Roushayd, with Kahyasi taking over late on. No sooner had Frankie made his move when Tony Ives on Emmson squashed Frankie tight against the rails. The plan was in ruins. Every time Frankie tried to get out he would be boxed in by another horse. Fortunately it made little difference in the grand scheme of things because Kahyasi was well below form and only managed to finish sixth.

By November, the end of the season, Frankie headed back to California, where he would spend his second successive winter. With his profile rapidly rising in Britain it was a chance for him to escape to somewhere he was a complete unknown. In California, he was just one of many foreign workers, and this allowed him to continue to develop his riding skills away from the glare of the British media. He managed to pick up a few minor race rides that winter, but that stay in California will probably be best remembered for the single enemy he made there.

One day after work, he approached leading American trainer Wayne Lukas, introduced himself, and offered to ride out for him whenever he was needed. Lukas looked him up and down, and replied, 'We're in good shape right now.' Frankie has never forgiven Lukas for that put-down. In the intervening years he has been hired by high-profile American trainers such as Charlie Whittingham and Bobby Frankel, but he has never offered his services to Lukas since.

Upon returning to Britain in the spring Frankie discovered he'd been installed as 3-1 favourite to be champion apprentice, raising his profile within the racing fraternity still further.

Before the season started, Frankie discovered he needed a new agent after Cliff Woof, who had booked his rides the previous season, had become too busy since he'd signed several more jockeys onto his books.

His friend Mattie Cowing, with whom he had built up such a rapport in Cuthie Suttle's betting shop, had turned Frankie down when he'd asked him to book his rides the previous season, dismissing Frankie as a wild, undisciplined rascal. But Bruce Raymond had had a word in Mattie's ear and this time round he accepted Frankie's offer. As with Peter Burrell, Frankie's relationship with Mattie was always based on friendship rather than business.

Despite their friendship, however, Mattie always took his professional duties seriously. He converted his spare bedroom into an office, and Frankie invested in a computer for him to make life easier. Each morning Mattie would ring round to book rides, building relationships with trainers and owners. But some things never change – by lunchtime he would head to Cuthie Suttle's betting shop where he would waste his afternoon, and usually his money!

The season really began to take off on 13 May at Newmarket, when Frankie rode Didicoy to victory in a valuable sprint race shown live on Channel 4. Later that afternoon he won again, narrowly, on Khaydara, sealing his place as a familiar name amongst racing fans.

June was to be a memorable month for Frankie. He was given a ride on Versailles Road, trained by Susan Piggott, wife of Lester. She had taken over his training licence while he served time at Her Majesty's Pleasure for tax evasion. Frankie won that race at Leicester, using up his 5 pounds claim in the process, in a memorable day in which he did a treble. Two more trebles followed before the month was over. Frankie could do no wrong.

And when Ray Cochrane broke his collarbone in a horrendous multi-horse pile-up at Doncaster, Frankie inherited rides on some of Luca's better horses. Although it was a terrible time for Ray, it was a boost for Frankie at the time, as it greatly increased his chances of winning the apprentices title. It was an opportunity he had to seize with both hands.

The first such test came at Lingfield on 15 July when Frankie rode Markofdistinction to a convincing victory. A few days later he found himself riding Versailles Road to victory once again, this time at Beverley. Lester

Piggott had phoned the office at Beverley prior to the race to hand some advice to Frankie about how to handle the horse, but a crackling phone line, combined with Frankie's relatively poor command of English, and Lester's well-known tendency to mutter, meant the advice didn't count for much. Fortunately, it didn't matter, as Frankie rode Versailles Road to an unchallenged victory. But one unfortunate consequence of this win was that his weight allowance was now completely used up and from now on he would be challenging his heroes on level terms. The impact of this shouldn't be underestimated as many a star apprentice has vanished into oblivion the moment this safety net is removed.

A bad month followed, Frankie couldn't do anything right. He was pipped at the post at many a race; he made some bad choices when it came to picking race meetings; and his fragile confidence took an enormous dent. He was beginning to seriously question whether he had what it took to succeed without the claim allowance.

Things picked up towards the end of August when Frankie's lead at the top of the apprentices' table became unassailable. He rode a treble at Goodwood, which included his first Group race win on legal Case in the Select Stakes.

His first Classic ride came at the St Leger, which had been switched to Ayr from Doncaster following of the accident involving Ray. Frankie rode NC Owen for Luca, but it was no fairytale, as the horse struggled on the mud and they finished well back.

This proved only a blip and Frankie was soon back to winning ways at the meeting now known as the Festival of British racing at Ascot, at which he added three more victories to the tally, which included recording his one-hundredth success on Chummy's Favourite in the Group 3 Krug Diadem Stakes. Frankie had made a name for himself in a significant race at a major racecourse in front of a packed stand.

He sealed the apprentice championship with a total of 75 wins, thus equalling the post-war record set by Edward Hide in 1956. However, before the season's end, there was to be another, more significant event that would propel Frankie to the front pages of the racing papers.

Ray Cochrane had made the surprise announcement that he would be leaving Luca Cumani at the end of the season to ride for Guy Harwood in 1990. Frankie was initially saddened to be losing Ray from the yard, and had greatly valued his advice, encouragement, and, on times, well-deserved bollockings. Some argued though that Ray had become a victim of Frankie's success, and that Frankie's rapid progress had prompted his decision to leave.

The racing papers were pretty certain Frankie would be appointed as Ray's successor, but there were logical reasons his appointment was no dead cert. Frankie was still only eighteen and his riding education was far from complete. He was still relatively inexperienced and being stable jockey would obviously entail a huge amount of responsibility.

The news was broken to Frankie by his father in a

telephone conversation. Frankie could tell by the unusually excitable tone of his father's voice that he had good news. It turned out Gianfranco had held extensive discussions with Luca over the previous few days and they'd hammered out a deal. Frankie would be stable jockey for the 1990 season.

Gone were the days of Gianfranco being a cold, distant father to Frankie. Now he was unwaveringly proud of his son and what he had achieved in such a remarkably short space of time and was quick to hand out plenty of advice to his son and heir. He also shared his one concern that this enormous responsibility had come a year too soon. One thing was for sure, the time for fooling around was well and truly over.

Not all coverage of the appointment was entirely flattering. *The Sun* chose to compare Frankie's passion for chocolate mousse with Ray's routine of running up to four miles a day to control his weight at 8st 4lb.

The day after the news became public Frankie was called into Luca's office, the very same office which had been the scene of many a harsh telling-off over the past few years. Luca lectured Frankie at length about the retainers and horses he could expect to ride from now on. The only slight dampener was that one or two owners were not entirely convinced of Frankie's ability and they reserved the right to choose a top jockey in important races – the onus was on Frankie to silence his critics.

With the season at an end, Frankie took some time out to learn to drive, which would certainly come in handy the following year, as up to now he had been hitching lifts with other jockeys and if that wasn't possible he'd pay out of his own pocket for one of the other lads to drive him.

Andy Keates had taught him the basics in the car park at Newmarket, which progressed to Andy giving him driving lessons round Newmarket town in the £200 Mazda Frankie had bought that summer. Once again Frankie's over-confident side came to the surface, and on a few occasions when he couldn't hitch a lift he removed the 'L' plates, took a chance, and drove himself. He seems to have been little concerned that had been caught it would surely have put an end to his ambitions as a jockey.

At the end of the season, Frankie took an intensive driving course with a firm in Manchester and managed to pass on his second attempt.

A few weeks later he'd be off to California for his third successive winter, but not before a fortnight's holiday with Colin Rate. The first week was spent in Colin's home town of Sunderland, drinking beer and generally causing havoc. Yet again, this was a recipe for Frankie to take things too far.

On the way home from a night out, Frankie and Colin headed to a kebab house. Behind them in the queue were a young couple. Frankie couldn't take his eyes off the young lady, her boobs being at his eye level didn't help matters! He said something in Italian to her boyfriend, which unfortunately for Frankie he understood perfectly. As a result both Frankie and Colin were sent flying through the open door onto the middle of the road. A brief glimpse of Frankie's sensible side surfaced when he persuaded Colin not to go back for a fight. Due to the difference in height and weight it would almost certainly have been a mismatch. Frankie's diplomacy paid off and Colin duly retreated from the confrontation.

But Frankie the risktaker put in a reappearance just a few minutes later. When they were struggling to find a cab, one of Colin's mates, armed with a screwdriver, forced open the door of a car, fiddled with the wires under the bonnet, and started the engine. He invited Frankie and Colin to jump in, which they foolishly did, and were given a lift home to Colin's house.

Clearly Frankie's reckless streak was far from gone. Being stable jockey for a leading trainer was not enough in itself to make him see the error of his ways and treat the job with the respect and responsibility it needed, a problem which would re-surface in the next few years with devastating consequences for Frankie's career.

After spending the second week repaying Colin's hospitality by taking him to his home in Milan, Frankie headed for the States once again.

Frankie had signed up with agent Bob Meldahl for that winter's racing, and he had managed to book Frankie some decent rides. Then, two days before Christmas, with Gianfranco and Christine watching eagerly from the stands, Frankie rode his first winner in the States on the appropriately-named Smart Dollars in a $27,000 race at Hollywood Park, knocking high-profile American jockey Laffit Pincay into second place in the process.

When he got back to the jockeys' room, it was time for the inevitable initiation ceremony, which wasn't so different from the one he had to endure when he first arrived at Newmarket. The jockeys crowded around him, tore off all his clothes and smothered his private parts with hoof oil. He was now one of the family.

The winning horse's trainer, the eccentric Chris Speckert, took Frankie and his entourage to a celebratory meal at his favourite restaurant in Sierra Madre.

Despite the temptation to build on his success in America, Frankie returned to Britain earlier than usual to make the most of the opportunity Luca had given him. He gave Frankie a £15,000 retainer for first claim on his services. Frankie decided to invest this, along with an extra £4,000 from his savings, on a grey Mercedes 190E to replace his decaying Mazda, and hired Andy Keates to be his full-time driver, a role he maintains to this day.

The new daily routine involved Frankie and Andy dragging Mattie Cowing away from Cuthie Suttle's betting shop and heading to the race meeting Frankie was riding in. This gave Mattie the opportunity to build up a rapport with the trainers he spoke to on the phone almost daily, and created more business in the process.

The season got off to the worst possible start for Frankie, through no fault of his own. After riding a few minor winners early on, he rode Long Island at Epsom's spring meeting. In the final furlong, Frankie was thrown to the ground, escaping uninjured, though severely shaken. The horse was not so lucky, she hit the rails before somersaulting through them and breaking her hind leg – in the end she had to be put down.

The subsequent stewards' inquiry placed the blame firmly on Michael Hills on Flying Diva for running into the back of them, earning him a 14-day suspension.

After the happy interlude of winning his first Group 2 race on Markofdistinction at Sandown, further bad luck followed. One day, late in May, Frankie was asleep on the back seat of his Mercedes as they headed for Haydock, when an almighty thud threw him to the floor behind the front seats. He managed to crawl out onto the motorway only to discover a large white van had crashed so hard into the back that the boot had been completely crushed. Had the accident happened in the Mazda, Frankie probably wouldn't have escaped with his life.

They say bad luck comes in threes, and the trio was completed three days later when he took a heavy fall on a horse called Muirfield Village at Sandown. The horse escaped uninjured, but Frankie was stretchered into an ambulance. Some things never change, and his new status as stable jockey didn't make him immune from Luca's rantings.

Luca warned Frankie that by riding as he had on Muirfield Village he would hurt other horses by cutting through their hind legs, which, in his eyes, was unforgivable. In other words, Frankie was so cocky with his riding that he was allowing his horse to gallop too close to those in front. Luca made it clear that he didn't mind if Frankie hurt himself, but hurting the horses was not acceptable.

The season improved when Royal Ascot came around and Frankie won the first race of the meeting on Markofdistinction in the Queen Anne Stakes, matching his father's achievement in 1975 on Imperial March. The winning tally continued in earnest and he managed to win his hundredth race of the season at Chepstow on 27 August, riding Line of Thunder to a smart victory. Frankie had become the first teenager since Lester Piggott, thirty-five years earlier, to reach that illustrious milestone.

Shortly afterwards Frankie rode a winner on Henryk, owned by Barney Curley, one of racing's most colourful and controversial characters, who is usually seen with a wide-brimmed hat accompanied by a neatly trimmed moustache. Barney had been a regular at Cuthie's betting shop in the early days – this is where he had got to know Frankie. He's made a substantial living over many years from professional gambling.

Barney is probably best known to the general public for selling his Georgian mansion in Ireland through the unorthodox method of a nationwide raffle. A complex character, a man of walking contradictions, and the enemy of the bookmaking establishment, Barney is a man with few real friends. But Frankie is one such exception, and winning for Barney that day clearly meant a great deal to Frankie.

Despite the aura of controversy that surrounds Barney, nobody can deny the enormous good work that he has done through DAFA (Direct Aid for Africa), the charity he set up and donated all profits from his autobiography towards. Frankie has donated heavily to the cause without drawing attention to his generosity and takes a keen interest in the charity's work. He is intent on travelling to Zambia at some point in the future, to witness first-hand the problems that exist there and the valuable work DAFA has done to improve the lives of its inhabitants.

The 1990 season brought its share of bad luck for Frankie, but he hadn't seen the last of his misfortune, when, on 8 September, he had just been beaten at Haydock on My Lord by Baylis. As they began to pull up, Baylis caught the heels of My Lord, sending Frankie crashing to the ground. He was quickly fitted with a neck brace by the paramedics and taken to a local hospital.

Luckily, the X-rays showed no fractures, and Frankie was soon sent home to recuperate. He wasn't well enough to face the long journey back to Newmarket, so Luca sent Donald McCain, son of Ginger, to pick Frankie up and take him to his parents' home in nearby Southport. Frankie seized the opportunity to meet three-times Grand National winner Red Rum, now enjoying his well-earned retirement.

That summer Frankie survived three falls that could easily have ended his career before it had really begun. Bad luck in one way, but very good luck in another. Frankie's temporary injuries from that final fall at Haydock were soon put into perspective when he received devastating news from Italy shortly afterwards. His close friend and fellow jockey, Marco Paganini, the young champion jockey of Italy, had been killed in a freak fall at Grosseto. The fall itself wasn't especially bad, but as he tried to get up he was kicked in the head by a backmarker.

Frankie was severely shaken by the news. Marco had been an enormous inspiration and source of encouragement for him when he began riding in Naples. The loss of such a close friend gave him a grim reminder of the very real risks his chosen profession brings.

He returned to the saddle in late September, when he finally managed to win a Group 1 race, riding Markofdistinction to a memorable victory, beating legends such as Steve Cauthen and Pat Eddery in the process. He turned this victory into a Group 1 double in the next race when he rode Shamshir to victory. There would be no time to celebrate, however, as he had to catch a flight to Canada to ride Shellac for Luca in a valuable race in Toronto the next day, in which they were beaten by a nose.

Not long afterwards, rumours started doing the rounds that the newly-freed Lester Piggott, at the grand old age of fifty-five, was planning a riding comeback to combat boredom and frustration latter middle age was bringing. Nobody seriously believed the Lester Piggott who dominated racing in the sixties and seventies still had it in him to compete at the highest level. He couldn't return to his winning ways of old... could he?

But it wasn't long before Lester silenced his critics, winning on Nicholas, trained by his wife Susan at Chepstow. He turned it into a double in the next race on Shining Jewel. The old man was back, and as good as ever.

Lester flew to America on Concorde to compete in the Breeders' Cup meeting at Belmont Park. He got into the country by telling immigration officials the purpose of his visit was pleasure, believing they wouldn't let him in for business purposes because he'd served a prison sentence for tax evasion. There's no doubt Lester certainly meant business come the day of the Breeders' Cup mile. He was riding Royal Academy. Frankie also took part riding Markofdistinction, but this was to be Lester's day. He made use of all his skills to ride Royal Academy to victory a whole head in front of Itsallgreektome. For once, Markofdistinction failed to get going and Frankie could only watch Lester's thrilling victory from a distance.

Frankie exceeded his expectations that year by riding 141 winners, beaten only by Steve Cauthen, Willie Carson and Pat Eddery, who became the first jockey since 1952 to ride a double century, totalling an incredible 209 wins. With the season at an end, it was time to go to California for the winter once more.

With his name now firmly established in Britain, Frankie's American agent Bob Meldahl managed to book him a series of decent rides, which gave him six winners over just a few weeks. Frankie stayed in California until the end of the season at Hollywood Park and then flew to Tuscany for a holiday with his family immediately after Christmas.

Upon his return, he made his debut on the long-running television quiz *A Question of Sport*. He was joined by snooker legend Steve Davis and team captain Ian Botham, whilst the opposition was made up of, team captain Bill Beaumont, goalkeeper Chris Woods and hurdler Kay Morley. In the lounge before filming, Frankie was enjoying a few drinks with Ian when someone tipped him off that one of the picture questions was Gianfranco winning the 1977 Irish Guineas on Pampapaul in a tight finish alongside Lester Piggott on The Minstrel. Frankie was a natural on the programme, and the banter he had with Ian and presenter David Coleman proved a valuable training ground for his time as team captain which would come years later. But back then the programme was a far more sombre affair and much of the banter was removed from the final cut.

During that winter, Luca's stable was rocked by the news that the Aga Khan was removing all his horses from training in the country. This was brought about after his filly, Aliysa, trained by Michael Stoute, was disqualified after winning the previous year's Oaks at Epsom. The Aga Khan was furious and blamed the doping procedures used in Britain. This had a devastating impact for Luca, costing him forty-five of his best horses. It would be a long way back.

As a result, Frankie could not expect the same quality of rides on such a regular basis for the 1991 season and there was never going to be any chance he would overtake his previous season's score. Things were so bad that he couldn't even find a ride for the Derby that year, which meant that he would have to wait another twelve months before he could make his debut in the greatest race of all.

His season only really got going in July when Mattie

booked him a ride on what was considered a no-hoper in the German Derby called Temporal. The hot favourite for the race was Lomitas, something of a superstar in Germany. Nobody believed Frankie stood a chance on Temporal, and with the horse's poor record, they should have been right.

The race got off to a promising start, but he was forced wide by Michael Roberts on Leone. It turned out to be an advantage because the going was better there. Lomitas looked like winning until Frankie charged past on Temporal, winning by half a length. The crowd couldn't believe what they had just witnessed. The script had been tossed out of the window, as had the formbook. Nobody could have predicted a young jockey based in Britain riding a poor horse could have beaten the mighty Lomitas. Frankie had been propelled onto the international stage in a major way.

His biggest win of the season in Britain came when he won the Sussex Stakes on Second Set at Glorious Goodwood, but there were to be no winners in any of the summer's major races.

Frankie managed to win a race named after him at Chepstow at the end of August on Mata Cara, after Frankie successfully twisted Luca's arm into letting him ride one of the stable's better horses in what was, for Frankie, a prestigious race. Frankie was awarded this honour after he rode his century there the previous season. Since not many teenagers have races named after them, Frankie was keen to put in a good show and in the end he won comfortably.

The Breeders' Cup mile was once again

disappointing for Frankie that October when his ride, Second Set, failed to make an impact in a race dominated by Opening Verse. A consolation prize of sorts came the following day when he won a valuable handicap for Luca on Shaima at Belmont Park.

The following month Frankie finally broke his duck in France, riding John Gosden-trained Susurration to victory at Saint-Cloud.

Despite this small mercy, there was no denying that, in Britain at least, this had been a severely disappointing season for Frankie. He ended the season in seventh place in the jockey's table with ninety-four winners. In spite of Mattie working frantically to book Frankie rides wherever he could, Luca losing so many high-quality horses the previous winter had inevitably taken its toll. Frankie's meteoric rise to the top had hit the buffers.

Inevitably, frustration began to set in and for the first time he began to consider the possibility that he might not be riding for Luca forever. He held talks with the late prolific owner Robert Sangster who wanted to lay second claim on Frankie's services after Luca. Talks broke down when Robert made it clear that Frankie would not be riding his two star horses, Rodrigo de Triano or the Henry Cecil-trained unbeaten filly Musicale. Robert was keen to remain loyal to Willie Carson who had already enjoyed considerable success on Rodrigo and wanted to use his own stable jockey on Musicale.

Frankie was also very aware of how close Robert was

to Lester Piggott, in a successful working relationship dating back many years. With Lester back riding and in good form, Frankie was conscious of the possibility Robert could ditch Frankie in favour of Lester whenever it suited him. Frankie and Robert became close friends in his final years, but at this time Frankie did not want to be playing second fiddle to anyone and no deal was ever reached.

For the first time in five years, Frankie did not spend the winter in California, another sign that he was eager for fresh challenges. Instead he signed a one-month contract with a Hong Kong Jockey Club. Success was limited and he won just four of his twenty-five rides. Disappointingly the visit was best remembered for the £100 fine he received for chewing gum during a stewards' inquiry, which was given a quarter-page of coverage in the local paper. Yet, undeterred by the lack of success, or their intolerance of chewing gum, Frankie loved everything about being in Hong Kong – the style of racing, the culture, and the opportunities to party which were playing an increasingly important part in his life.

His debut in Japan was made the following March when he took part in the young jockeys' world championship at Nakayama. This would see Frankie pitted against leading young jockeys from all over the world, including the likes of local hero Yutaka Take, Corey Nakatani and Johnny Murtagh, all of whom would go on to make it at the highest level.

The title was contended over a series of races held that Sunday, and Frankie emerged overall winner.

HARD LESSONS

Once the meeting was over, Frankie attended the buffet dinner, where he had to endure endless speeches before every rider was presented with a variety of gifts such as cameras and watches. As title winner, Frankie earned the biggest prize of all, £20,000 in cash.

Little did Frankie know that he was on the brink of self-destruction and was in serious danger of throwing his career away.

CHAPTER 6

Enjoying the High Life

Frankie's dedication to riding seemed to be waning somewhat by now. He had begun to enjoy the trappings fame and fortune brings, and, like many men his age, wanted to party as hard and as often as possible.

Alarm bells started ringing in Luca's ears following Frankie's win in the German Derby. That night in Hamburg Frankie hit the town hard, and headed for the red light district, where he jumped through an open window to take a look at what was on offer. By the time he staggered back to the hotel, it was daylight.

He crashed onto the bed and missed his flight home to Britain, where he was due to be riding for Luca that afternoon. When he finally woke up and realised the time, he panicked, and rang Luca's pilot, Neil Foreman, who agreed to fly to Hamburg from Newmarket to pick Frankie up, dropping him off at Leicester where he'd hopefully arrive in time for the third race.

In early 1992 Frankie bought a place of his own, which on the surface may have seemed a natural enough development, but in reality removed him from the watchful eye of his landlady Bernice and left him free to go off the rails. He frequently gave in to temptation, going out boozing with his friends when he should have been on a strict diet and in bed early ready for the following day's racing.

Without a landlady or other mother-figure to watch over him, Frankie was free to bring girls back to his flat as often as he liked. And there were lots of them. Colin Rate stayed at the flat now and again and was quick to pass comment on Frankie's taste in women.

One lady who alleges she was on the scene around this time is the former *Emmerdale* and *Bad Girls* actress, Claire King. In her autobiography she speaks of an on-off romance lasting two years, which was probably starting to wind down by the time the 1992 season got into swing.

Her account of her romance with Frankie, and numerous other men, including his close friend Vinnie Jones, reads like a Mills and Boon novel and leaves little to the imagination when judging their sexual performances. She claims they first met when David Craig, the former jockeys' agent, who is now a presenter on *Sky Sports News*, drove her to Newmarket where she was first introduced to Mattie, whom she remembers fondly, before being driven on to Frankie's place.

According to her account, from the moment Frankie opened the door, there was an attraction between the pair. They then sat in the living room having drinks where she claims they couldn't take their eyes off each other. She states that Frankie thought David was Claire's boyfriend at first, but once she subtly hinted he wasn't the coast was clear for them.

The four of them then set off in Mattie's car for a meal in The Plough, a trendy restaurant near Newmarket. Claire claimed there was a real spark between them as they sat opposite each other during the meal. On the way back, Mattie and David sat in the front of the car whilst she and Frankie sat in the back. She states that Frankie started kissing her passionately on the journey home, and upon arriving back at Frankie's she allowed him to lead her to bed.

According to Claire, the following morning, Frankie brought her breakfast in bed when he arrived back from riding out, after which they swapped phone numbers and agreed to meet up soon. According to her, they'd meet up whenever Frankie was riding up north. The relationship came to an end when she developed feelings for fellow *Emmerdale* actor, Peter Amory, whom she obviously saw far more frequently. Claire claims the last time she saw Frankie was during a trip to Santa Anita to visit an old friend. Whilst she was there she took the chance to meet up with Frankie who was out there riding.

Whatever the reality, Claire tells a quite plausible story about Frankie's wild behaviour – it fits perfectly with the sort of thing he was doing at that time. She alleges one night Frankie turned up totally unannounced at her house in Yorkshire. However, his timing wasn't great as she'd already promised to take her friend and her mother to see the Chippendales in Harrogate. She told Frankie to amuse himself whilst she was gone. When she returned it was all quiet downstairs, so she went upstairs only to find Frankie passed out on the bed with an empty bottle of wine next to him and champagne in the chiller. This was bad enough in itself, but Frankie had gone to the trouble of creating a romantic scene, with rose petals scattered over the sheets and candles around the bed. Yet, by the time Claire had returned, she claims, the candles had all but melted and if she'd arrived slightly later the house would've been on fire.

One thing is certain – by 1992 there were too many things distracting Frankie from riding, and his commitment level was nowhere near as high as it had been six years earlier when he had first arrived in Britain.

Plenty of other young sports stars enjoy the high life too much and soon fade into oblivion, and there was a very real danger Frankie was going the same way. He didn't know it at the start of the season, but this would be his last riding for Luca. Over the next few months, his behaviour would push his employer too far.

Things seemed to be going well when Frankie was given the chance to ride in his first Epsom Derby by John Gosden. He'd been asked to mount Pollen Count, who seemed to have a good chance, thanks to winning the Thresher Classic Trial at Sandown, ridden by Steve Cauthen. When Steve received a better offer for the big race, John turned to Frankie to ride Pollen Count. But, to set the standard for the years that would follow, Frankie's horse disappointed on the day. Pollen Count came in third from last, after leading early in the race before burning out completely.

However, the very next day, Frankie received an unexpected boost thanks to one of his father's contacts, the French bloodstock agent Robert Nataf, who asked Frankie to ride an outsider called Polytain in the French Derby. The horse felt good on the way to the start, and Frankie told Steve Cauthen he thought the horse was underrated, a claim Steve laughed off.

They spent most of the race sat comfortably in sixth, then Frankie gave him some encouragement as they turned for home. Frankie pulled him out in the final one and a half furlongs where the horse began charging to the front, sealing an incredible, and entirely unexpected victory in the style of a true champion.

Frankie seemed to be on a roll as Royal Ascot began, where he rode a superb horse in Drum Taps in the Gold Cup. His main competition was likely to come from Arcadian Heights, who had something of a reputation as a bloodthirsty horse, following an incident at Newmarket where he bit the top off David Loder's little finger.

The Gold Cup takes place over two and a half miles, a huge distance for a flat race. The best thing Frankie could do was make the horse switch off as soon as possible once the race was underway, conserving all energy for the final few furlongs. Things went to plan at first, but as the race progressed Frankie sensed Drum Taps was becoming increasingly impatient, and so let him run once they were on the straight.

Soon after, Frankie became aware of Walter Swinburn on Arcadian Heights closing in on him. Swinburn's ride soon lived up to his reputation by trying to take a chunk out of Frankie's backside. Fortunately for Frankie, Drum Taps quickened up in time and won by two lengths. Subsequent footage showed just how close Frankie came to being bitten by Arcadian Heights in the final stages of the race, and stewards ordered that the horse must be fitted with a net muzzle for future races.

In another of the few highlights of the season, Frankie rode Gold Medal for Martin Pipe in his one and only race over hurdles at Chepstow – an annual contest between flat and jump jockeys. Frankie was utterly petrified of jumping hurdles, something he'd never done before in his life, so sought advice from Richard Dunwoody, who told him the only thing he needed to worry about was making sure his horse had a decent view before he jumped every hurdle.

Frankie had lied to Pipe by telling him he had experience over hurdles, but inside he was anything but confident, terrified of the prospect of undertaking this dangerous, and completely different challenge. For him, this was like going on a massive rollercoaster ride without wearing a safety belt. But by now, it was too late to turn back.

In an attempt to give off a false aura of confidence, he rode to the start with his knees under his chin. It was only once he arrived at the start that he realised that the stirrups he was using would only drop down two holes, leaving him unable to drop his leathers to a sensible length. It was far too late to do anything about it now, but the lack of control over the horse increased his fear tenfold.

With the rising of the tape, Gold Medal shot off at top speed. Frankie was powerless to control him as they approached the first hurdle, and he was totally panic-stricken by the prospect of having to jump the hurdle on a horse he had no control over – so he shut his eyes and hoped the moment would pass as quickly and as safely as possible. The horse got over the hurdle, but there was no time to relax as the second approached. Once they'd conquered this hurdle safely, Frankie began to relax slightly and his confidence levels increased, so, against his better judgement, he gave the horse a slap. The horse reacted by charging at full speed – which was disastrous with so much of the race still to go. Frankie, still feeling completely helpless, called out to Richard Dunwoody for some mid-race advice. He told him to sit further back and keep his legs out in front of him. It did the trick and Frankie and Gold Medal jumped the rest of the hurdles without mishap, but the horse had quickened up too early and was ultimately lucky to finish fourth. Traumatised by the experience, Frankie vowed to stick to flat racing in future and turned down the chance to ride in the race the following year, and every year since!

His only other big win that season came when he was riding Red Slippers for Luca in the Sun Chariot Stakes at Newmarket as the season drew to a close.

In a disappointing season, Frankie managed 101 winners in Britain, leaving him seventh in the jockey's table. This was in a large part due to Luca no longer having access to the quality of horses he enjoyed prior to the Aga Khan pulling out. Though it would be unfair to attribute all the blame on Luca's misfortune. Frankie's party lifestyle inevitably took its toll. He was turning up at race meetings hung-over in a tracksuit and trainers, rather than in the dapper suits he would have been seen in a few years earlier.

Frankie's relationship with Luca had never been an easy one, and Frankie being made stable jockey didn't improve the nature of the relationship in the way Frankie would have expected. He was never treated in the way Ray Cochrane had been when he was stable jockey. In Luca's eyes, Frankie was still very much the naughty kid who'd arrived eight years earlier, and evidently this wasn't going to change anytime soon. Frankie was on the lookout for new challenges and knew his days riding for Luca were numbered.

In truth, Luca was probably right to treat Frankie the way he did. When he arrived, he was still a boy, and was treated as such. He was now a man, but not a responsible adult who treated the role of stable jockey with the seriousness it deserved. He was the antithesis of the dedication and discipline shown by his predecessor, Ray Cochrane, and was treated accordingly by Luca.

Frankie began his search for a new challenge by flying to Hong Kong upon the conclusion of the flat season in Britain, accepting a one-month contract with the Hong Kong Jockey Club, as he had done the previous winter. But things didn't go according to plan – racing was cancelled for four weeks due to an outbreak of horse sickness. This gave Frankie time to indulge in his biggest passion at the time-partying. He lived the playboy lifestyle during those four weeks, out partying every night in one of the most dynamic cities in the world, having more than his share of girls along the way. He was seduced by the trappings being a jockey in Hong Kong brought. All his expenses were paid, the money was superb, and the lifestyle was in a different league to the one he had in Britain. The way he was feeling, he'd have loved to have stayed in Hong Kong for good.

And the opportunity to do just that arose when Gary Ng Ting-Keung, a prominent Hong Kong trainer who had some big owners behind him, approached Frankie with a view to signing him up. They discussed terms over long lunches and dinners at which Frankie was presented with several gold watches. Figures being banded about were in the region of a quarter of a million pounds over two years as a retainer. This was an offer Frankie surely couldn't refuse.

News of Frankie's plans to sign with Gary Ng were leaked to the press in early February, before he'd had the chance to break the news to Luca, a prospect he was understandably dreading. No contract had been signed at this stage because Gary hadn't yet been given permission by the Hong Kong Jockey Club to retain a stable jockey, nor had they approved Frankie's application to ride there full-time.

Meanwhile, in Britain, significant changes were taking place in the racing scene. Steve Cauthen had ended his role as Sheikh Mohammed's jockey, deciding to retire and return home to America. He was replaced by Michael Roberts, who had just become champion jockey for the first time.

Frankie returned to Britain in March, where he was forced to face the inevitable showdown with Luca, which was never going to be easy or pleasant. Frankie walked straight into his office and told him of his intentions. This brought out a side of Luca that Frankie had never before witnessed. Yes, he'd seen him angry before, but his anger had risen to a whole new altitude upon hearing this news first hand. Luca wasted no time in telling Frankie exactly what he thought of him and his shoddy attitude to the job, before taking just a few minutes out to try and persuade him to change his mind. Hong Kong, he believed, was a place where ageing jockeys made a quick buck in the autumn of their career, and Frankie had no business in that game.

But Frankie's mind was made up, and there was nothing Luca could say or do to change it. Luca switched back to his ultra-angry mode, telling Frankie he never wanted to see him again. A few days later, Frankie discovered Ray Cochrane would be returning to Luca as stable jockey. There would be no way back!

Meanwhile, Frankie had to look for spare rides to occupy his time before starting his new role in Hong Kong. He found a brief solace from his problems by winning the young jockeys' world championship for the second year in a row before the flat season began. But it wasn't long before he was brought back down to earth with the reality that this was going to be a tough season. Mattie was going to have to work flat out to find Frankie spare rides whenever and wherever he could, and Frankie would inevitably end up on far poorer horses than he'd been used to.

Confused and unhappy, Frankie continued to spend his nights clubbing and mixing with people who couldn't care less about the impact this lifestyle was having on his professional life. As the season wore on he started riding out for David Loder, who was making a name for himself as a fiercely ambitious young trainer, and who provided him with a few winners. Frankie had a handful of allies during this difficult period, such as Barney Curley and Reg Hollinshead, who would tried to raise his spirits, but times were tough.

Things started to improve slightly in mid April when he won the Group 3 John Porter Stakes at Newbury on 25-1 shot Linpac West, turning it into a double by winning the following race, the Greenham on Inchinor for Roger Charlton. The double became the treble when he won the Ladbrokes Spring Cup in the Queen's colours on Tissisat, trained by Ian Balding. Later that day he rode a fourth success on Winged Victory, in a day that gave a much-needed boost to his shattered confidence. But the impact of this stimulus was to be short lived. Frankie's world would soon come crashing down as never before.

The following day Frankie headed to Wembley to support his beloved Arsenal in the League Cup final. It should've been a great day. He and a group of mates from Newmarket set off in a minibus, along with a good supply of beer. And Frankie and Colin painted their faces in Arsenal's colours of red and white. They were dropped off near the ground but there was time for a few more pints in a nearby pub before heading for Wembley where they witnessed an emphatic Arsenal victory – they demolished Sheffield Wednesday 3-1.

After the game, they began their journey home to Newmarket when two of his accomplices decided they wanted to celebrate with a night out in London. It didn't take much to persuade Frankie to join them since he was enjoying the party lifestyle to the full and beyond during this period. The three of them jumped out at a set of lights and flagged down a taxi which took them to the centre of London. They set off on a huge pub crawl which eventually led to a club in Oxford Street. Frankie had never been much of a beer drinker, but today was the exception and by the time he arrived at the club he was completely out of it, and in the mood to try anything.

Someone came up to his gang selling drugs, and Frankie gave into temptation and bought a small amount of cocaine. Hours later, he was messing around with his mates outside a club in Falconberg Mews when they were approached by two policemen carrying torches. They began to question them. At worst Frankie feared being told to cool down for being drunk and disorderly. Without warning, the police asked all three of them to turn out their pockets. His mates were clean, but Frankie still had a small quantity of cocaine in his pocket from earlier. He'd completely forgotten it was there, but actions have consequences and it didn't take long for Frankie to sober up after rediscovering the contents.

He was arrested, thrown into the back of a van and taken to the nearest police station. He began to contemplate what the impact of this incident might be. He feared he might lose his liberty, and knew this could well spell the end of his career.

Upon arriving at the police station, he was searched

again, had his fingerprints taken, and was made to tell them where he had bought the cocaine from. After a lengthy period on his own in the interview room, Frankie was bailed and told to return in three weeks. He was naturally relieved to be out but he knew this was far from the end of the matter, and inevitably, the fallout from it had only just begun.

He was left to find his own way back to Newmarket from the police station when he was released in the early hours, but managed to flag down a taxi to take him home. The first person Frankie had to face in the morning was Colin, who was shocked and disappointed in his best friend's actions. If he had been there, it almost certainly would not have happened.

But there was not time to dwell on the previous night's events as Frankie was due to ride at Nottingham that afternoon. On the way there all sorts of thoughts entered Frankie's head. The Jockey Club had just introduced random dope testing of jockeys and he speculated privately there was a fair chance he'd fail if he was required to give a sample that day. In the end, he wasn't tested, though with his mind elsewhere he drew a blank in the saddle. The following morning the tabloids had found out what had happened and wasted no time in giving the story maximum exposure. Frankie, ashamed and embarrassed, didn't know if he could continue at all.

One inevitable piece of bad news arrived within a few days. The whole Hong Kong deal was well and truly off. The Hong Kong authorities were never overly keen on allowing him to take up his contract with Gary

Ng and this episode gave them the excuse they needed to stop it happening.

During the bail period Frankie rode terribly. He wasn't sleeping well, fearing the consequences when he returned to the police station, and his mind was in a daze when he was riding. This period brought him a seven-day ban for careless riding at Leicester followed shortly afterwards by a four day ban for improper use of the whip at Newmarket in the 1,000 Guineas. Ironically, the horse Frankie rode in that race was Dayflower, his first mount for what was the forerunner of the mighty Godolphin stable.

With the day of reckoning fast approaching, Gianfranco flew in to give his son support at this difficult time. Frankie felt ashamed that he'd let his father down, but the response he received from Gianfranco wasn't as harsh as he feared. Once he realised his son was genuinely remorseful, he told him he must learn a lesson from what had happened. This was an exercise in damage limitation, so Gianfranco began by persuading his son to hire a solicitor.

On 10 May, Frankie's bail was up and he arrived at Marylebone police station, where several of the paparazzi were already waiting for him. His solicitor's plan was to get the police to issue Frankie with a caution for possession of a controlled drug. This would prevent the need for a court appearance and, from a legal point of view, bring closure to the matter.

But he was by no means sure that the plan would work. With Frankie so high-profile, there was a very real possibility that they would take the opportunity to make an example of him. They gathered in a room where the police made it clear to Frankie that if he was charged with another offence it would seriously affect his chances of getting a visa for working abroad. His solicitor then went to work, and an agreement was reached that Frankie would accept a police caution. A police caution was serious – there could be no repeat of this sort of thing – but it could have been so much worse. And he was allowed to leave via the back entrance to avoid the press pack at the front.

With his father on the scene to give him some much needed discipline, Frankie began to look to the future and began to focus on riding again, with determination that had been lacking in the previous few years. He started to ride out whenever his services were required and made his riding comeback, following his 11-day suspension on 14 May.

Frankie did not know what sort of reaction he would get when he arrived at Newbury that day. Things weren't as bad as they might have been. It goes without saying that the jockeys in the weighing room spent the afternoon winding him up about it, but there was also a great deal of sympathy from the owners and trainers he rode for.

Deep down, Frankie knew he couldn't carry on living the way he was and the arrest proved to be an important crossroads in his life. The week after his comeback, he found himself riding from Newmarket to Goodwood in a party that included Barney Curley. He said very little both there and back, hardly speaking until they were diverted to Cambridge on the way home.

As they drove away from the landing strip, Barney asked Frankie if he was serious about riding or just playing at it. He felt somewhat stung for being asked such a question, but assured Barney he was deadly serious about making it as a top jockey. So Barney invited Frankie round to his house in Stretchworth that night for a game of snooker. It was to change his life forever and brought out a side of Barney's character few of the general public have ever seen.

Barney left Frankie in no doubt as to where he was going wrong. He was convinced Frankie was riding badly, half-heartedly, as though he didn't care whether he won or lost. He told other home truths as well, such as the need for the late nights and wild, irresponsible behaviour to stop. It was hard for Frankie to argue with any of this. He knew every word Barney was saying was true, and significantly, he was the first to tell him so to his face.

Frankie spent the next few hours trying to persuade Barney he was still determined to make it as a top jockey and to change his ways. In the end, Barney offered him an olive branch. He made it clear to Frankie that it was up to him to prove he was serious about his riding, and if he did so, he'd do everything in his power to help him. Then Barney threw in a powerful incentive. He knew Frankie loved his beautiful home, and he told Frankie he would sell it to him if he ever became champion jockey. They swapped homes three years later!

Frankie thought long and hard about what Barney had said that evening. It was now up to him to put

Above: A jubilant Frankie Dettori, riding Markofdistinction, enters the winners' enclosure at Ascot after winning the Queen Elizabeth II Stakes in 1990, the year he burst into the UK racing scene.

Below: Frankie winning the same stakes nine years later with Dubai Millennium, the best horse he'd ever ridden.

Above left: Frankie also won the Dubai Cup on Dubai Millennium, in 2000. The winner's purse was a whopping $3.6m – $30,000 per second of the race.

Above right: Two of his staunchest supporters in life: his wife Catherine and his close friend and manager Peter Burrell.

Below: With his main employer Sheikh Mohammed, owner of the Godolphin stables.

Kissing outside the Catholic church in Newmarket where Frankie and Catherine got married on a fine Sunday in July 1997.

With the family: Frankie, Catherine, Leo and Ella at the film premiere of *The Chronicles of Narnia: The Lion, The Witch and The Wardrobe*, in 2006.

Above: Frankie with his friend Michael Owen, who owns his own stable of racehorses.

Below left: Playing around with ex-footballer Vinnie Jones, who was also managed by Peter Burrell.

Below right: With Rolling Stone Ronnie Wood at his Western-themed 50th birthday party. Being a real racing enthusiast they became good friends with Ronnie playing guitar at Frankie's wedding reception.

Showing his trademark dismount leap up for joy after winning the Hong Kong Cup on Fantastic Light in 2000.

Above: The wreckage of the plane that crashed on that fateful day in June 2000, injuring Frankie and fellow jockey Ray Cochrane, and tragically killing regular Godolphin pilot Patrick Mackey.

Below left: Showing the extent of his facial injuries from the crash.

Below right: Frankie with Ray at Patrick's funeral. Although neither were in a fit state to travel, they were both keen to pay their respects to their friend.

Above: Frankie Dettori on Atlantis Prince leading the field as he wins the Tote Exacta Condition Stakes at Newmarket on his return to racing after the plane crash, August 5 2000.

Below: Showing his relief in the winners' enclosure after his triumphant comeback.

things right. True to his word, Barney played a vital role in persuading John Gosden to give him a chance. This, in turn, would ultimately open the door to Sheikh Mohammed and the Godolphin operation. But that was in the future. First, there was ground work to be done.

He listened hard to his father, who told him to stop talking to the press for now and focus purely on his riding. When Derby day arrived Frankie had only ridden sixteen winners all season. That day at Epson Frankie won the opening race on Moccasin Run, turning it into a double as he triumphed on Enharmonic in the Diomed Stakes in the Queen's colours, on the fortieth anniversary of her coronation.

Things didn't go so well in the Derby itself. Frankie was riding Wolf Prince for American trainer Michael Dickinson, which never really stood a chance in a race won by Commander in Chief.

But Frankie enjoyed further success when the Ascot Gold Cup came around, winning for the second year in succession on Drum Taps. And with the help of Mattie working flat out to find Frankie spare rides, the season started to turn round. He rode Lochsong to an unchallenged victory at the Sandown Eclipse meeting in early July, and won again on the horse at Goodwood after a scrap with Paris House in the Group 3 King George Stakes

In August, the horses would go head to head once more in the Nunthorpe Stakes at York. Frankie suspected five furlongs might be a bit much for her, so made her run flat out in the early stages to give her as much of a lead as possible. This time there was no competition. Lochsong was in charge throughout, leaving Paris House trailing way behind. Frankie's new-found dedication was starting to pay off.

Shortly afterwards in Deauville, the season got even better – in fact, Frankie had a magical day, winning two valuable races. The first victory came on Prince Babar, followed by a second on Dana Springs. Both races were worth over £170,000 to the winning owner, for which Frankie took a percentage in what was a very nice day's work.

Frankie was working hard to restore his reputation, but there was still a long way to go. Whenever he and Luca were at the same meeting, they blanked each other and the rift was as deep as it had been in the spring. But Barney was certain that Frankie apologising to Luca was a crucial step in putting things right, so he took steps on Frankie's behalf to make it happen.

When Barney first approached Luca, he was told not to bother. Luca, whilst a stubborn character, felt justifiably let down by the way Frankie had treated him that spring and didn't feel the urge to be reconciled with Frankie. But Barney kept his promise to Frankie to do everything he could to help him, provided he started to take his riding seriously. He harassed Luca until he relented, and one wet evening in late August, Frankie turned up at Luca's door. He knocked on the door, terribly nervous about the encounter. Luca answered, Frankie gave a reluctant grin, and asked Luca if he could come in. Luca told him to wait, and shut the door in his face, leaving Frankie to get wet. It was Luca's way of making sure

Frankie suffered for a bit longer, but Frankie's attitude had changed, and he was now prepared to wait for as long as it took to put things right. A few minutes later, Luca opened the door again, they shook hands, and proceeded to his office.

The first thing Frankie did was apologise for the way he had left Luca earlier in the season, conceding that his behaviour had been arrogant and childish. Then he went on to try and persuade Luca he really had changed for the better. The conversation didn't last long, but at least the first step had been taken. Then came the catch. As Frankie was leaving, Luca told him he wouldn't be using his services for at least another year. Luca believed only time would prove whether Frankie really had changed.

By now Barney was in no doubt that Frankie had re-dedicated himself to riding and was a changed man. There were no signs of him returning to his old ways, so, true to form, he kept his promise to help him out in any way he could.

Michael Roberts' deal to ride Sheikh Mohammed's horses wasn't going as well as expected. It wasn't really his fault, as he was being asked to do an impossible job – with several of the Sheikh's trainers wanting his services at the same time, which inevitably lead to friction. He was being expected to ride over six hundred horses for over twenty trainers in all – far too much to ask of any jockey.

When Barney became aware of this he contacted John Gosden and suggested he take a serious look at Frankie. Aware of Frankie's much-chronicled problems in the not-too-distant past, John was apprehensive. He was no mug and wasn't going to be taken for a ride by Frankie or anybody else. But he took Barney's views seriously, and agreed to meet Frankie.

On the day of the meeting John made it clear that he wasn't prepared to put up with any of Frankie's old shenanigans, and he'd be quickly shown the door if those ways showed signs of reappearing. Shortly afterwards, John met the Sheikh to sort out the problems Michael Roberts was having with several trainers, all employed by the Sheikh. John proposed retaining a jockey to ride the Sheikh's horses he was responsible for. The Sheikh agreed to this arrangement, and the jockey John wanted for the role was Frankie.

It goes without saying that Frankie didn't need much persuading to accept the role. He had ridden for the Sheikh from time to time in the past, and was aware of his fiercely ambitious plans in British racing. The news broke in mid-September, at the same time as it was confirmed that Michael Roberts' contract was not being renewed.

The partnership got off to a good start as on that day Frankie rode the Sheikh's filly Arvola to victory at Nottingham. His old ways were now behind him and he was not going back to them. Not only had he been given a golden, once-in-a-lifetime opportunity as a jockey, his personal life was finally starting to settle down as well. By this stage, Frankie had met Catherine.

CHAPTER 7

Behind Every Great Man...

By the autumn of 1993, Frankie's wild days were well and truly behind him. He was on form, riding winners on an almost daily basis, and developing close links with Sheikh Mohammed and his principal trainer, John Gosden, which would soon lead to a lucrative contract for Frankie with Godolphin.

At the back of the minds of those closest to him was the fear that Frankie would soon slip back into his bad old ways of womanising and partying. A chance meeting with the woman that was to bring stability and contentment to his life was to put an end to their understandable worries once and for all.

In early September, Ian Balding took a gamble and entered Lochsong into the six furlong Group 1 Sprint Cup at Haydock, against his better judgement. Frankie suspected the horse was out of its depth over this distance and he was duly beaten by John Gosden's duo Wolfhound and Catrail in the last hundred yards.

Frankie boarded his last mount of the day, Azola, for David Loder, for whom he had been riding out in the mornings. A normally unwaveringly focussed Frankie was distracted by the young girl leading the horse round. Frankie vaguely recognised her from David Loder's yard, but he'd never had the chance to speak to her. He immediately broke the ice by using his well-rehearsed, cringeworthy chat up line, 'Allo darling, where have you been hiding?' He then asked her name, which was Catherine Allen. As they left the paddock he pestered her for a date.

At the time, Catherine was a nineteen year old student of Classical Studies at Surrey University. Her parents lived in Cambridge, and she often returned home midweek to ride out for David Loder. Her father, William (known as Twink) came to Britain as a young vet with his wife Diana. He had a scholarship to Cambridge and has remained there ever since, and is now a leading professor on equine fertility at Cambridge University.

The day Catherine met Frankie, she was standing in for one of the girls on holiday. She would not normally have been around on a race day. Catherine was initially reluctant to get involved with Frankie, having heard all the tales about his wild past. But after much pestering for her phone number on the way round to the start she finally relented, telling Frankie he'd forget it straight away anyway. Azola was beaten into third place, but as Catherine came out onto the course to lead her back, he recited her number successfully. Frankie had a date.

From the very beginning of the relationship the problems that Catherine would later have to get used were present. From the outset, a great deal of tolerance of Frankie's hectic diary was needed, along with an acceptance of his disciplined lifestyle. Frankie couldn't fit in a date that weekend because he had to ride in Florence that day, and the next weekend he was due back in Italy once again.

In the end, the first date was to a trip to the cinema in Cambridge, followed by a meal at Pizza Express. Unsurprisingly, Frankie did most of the talking on that first date, during which he casually remarked that he didn't appreciate women wearing make up. Catherine was clearly paying attention, as she has never worn make up, not even lipstick, since.

The relationship developed quickly, but the early courtship was far from easy. They'd arrange to meet up for a meal, then Frankie would ring at the last minute to call it off, citing being too tired or having to waste hard for a ride the next day. Sometimes, he'd drop her off at her parents' house early in the evening then head home to bed because he had to be up so early the next morning.

During the courtship, planning things proved consistently difficult. Frankie had the tendency to be a bit short with Catherine when he was tired. But she proved tolerant and understanding with him, and they soon became an item, although they both agreed Catherine should complete her degree course, which she duly did.

Ever the romantic, Frankie took Catherine on dates to Arsenal games at Highbury early on. This only stopped after a terrifying incident whilst queuing to collect their tickets for the derby game against Tottenham. A huge fight broke out in front of them between rival supporters. As mounted police and dog handlers moved in, Frankie and Catherine were sandwiched in the middle of the brawl, crushed against a wall of the stadium by the mob.

In the autumn of the 1993 season, Frankie's career was going from strength to strength, helped in no small part by his continuing success on Lochsong. In early September, the horse was stepped back up to six furlongs by trainer Ian Balding and responded well to the challenge, as Frankie rode her to a convincing victory in the Group 1 Sprint Cup at Haydock.

On the day of the Prix de l' Arc de Triomphe, Frankie was again on board Lochsong in the Prix de l'Abbaye. They got off to a roaring start, and soon built up a convincing lead. By the halfway stage, there was never any doubt as to the result.

In the final weeks of the season Frankie went from strength to strength, amazingly finishing runner up to Pat Eddery in the championship with 149 winners, which would have been unthinkable six months earlier.

Frankie's past briefly came back to haunt him when the Japan Racing Association hinted that they would not allow him entry to ride Misil in the Japan Cup due to their strict drug policy. But John Gosden's wife, a bright lawyer, advised Frankie to make a statement making it clear that he hadn't applied for a licence to ride in Japan and hadn't been denied one. The statement went on to say that commitments elsewhere would prevent him from riding in Japan.

His relationship with Catherine faced one of its most serious tests that December. Frankie was deadly serious about making the most of the winter all-weather programme, beginning in early January. After riding in Hong Kong, followed by a few days' holiday there, Frankie headed to his parents' house near Agadir in Morocco to prepare himself for the challenge that lay ahead.

During the next ten days, which included Christmas, everything was geared towards bringing Frankie to a peak of physical and psychological fitness for the hectic racing calendar which lay ahead the moment the festivities were over. Catherine had to take a back seat during this special time of year when couples expect to be together. She had to make do with phone calls every couple of days, coming a distant second to Frankie's disciplined preparations.

To describe Frankie's ten days in Morocco as hugely disciplined does not do his regime justice. He lived off a diet of grilled fish, a two-pounder, nearly always sea bass, eaten once a day, on its own, without oil, salad or potatoes. He mostly drank plain water, and the only alcohol he consumed was half a glass of champagne on Christmas Day.

Each day, he'd wake up around 10am, have one espresso with a sweetener, a large bottle of water, then sit in the sun until 2pm. He'd then put on his walkman and set off on a long, brisk walk along the beach towards Agadir and back again, covering ten miles in just over two hours.

During the last hour he'd have to overcome severe

hunger pains whilst walking and jogging, then he'd arrive home to a relaxing bath whilst his father cooked him his one, meanly-rationed meal of the day. After the meal, he'd set off on his bike to Agadir to ring Catherine.

Catherine's tolerance of Frankie's lifestyle was severely tested during this time. It required enormous sacrifice and understanding on her part, which surely could not have been easy for one so young. She was, in effect, being asked to make a firm commitment to a man she would only be able to see, or even speak to on the phone, when he had time to fit her in. Last minute cancellations and disappointments, not to mention severe mood swings, were all inconveniences she quickly learnt to accept.

At the same time, it also illustrates just how much Frankie had changed during the previous twelve months. Gone were the wild parties and womanising, and in came a focussed, disciplined rider with striking similarities to the father he had so revered and feared as a child. The stabling influence Catherine undoubtedly brought into his life certainly helped Frankie stay on the straight and narrow.

For as long as Catherine was around, there was never any danger of Frankie reverting to his wild days or bad habits. In her, he had found a personal contentment that helped him hold on to his new-found fierce dedication to riding. Both Catherine, and the new attitude he found in the autumn of that year, have remained constants in his life to this day.

Over the next three years, as Frankie's professional career began to bring him major success, his relationship with Catherine developed. She learnt exactly how to handle his mood swings, which can change from being hyperactively high to unbearably low. Catherine learnt how to lift his mood when he was down and bring him back down to earth when he was over the top.

At times, there is little doubt that she found being his partner frustrating, and as the next few years progressed, finding time to be together seldom got any easier. Her commitment to him, however, remained unwavering and this did not go unnoticed by Frankie, who decided it was time to take things a step further.

On Valentine's Day, 1996, Frankie took Catherine to lunch at his favourite Italian restaurant called Scalini, situated just behind Harrods. Once they had finished the main course, Frankie suggested Catherine place her napkin over her eyes. For a moment, she refused, but after a while she agreed to turn away. Frankie went down on one knee, took her hands, and asked Catherine to marry him. Sure enough she said yes. The diamond engagement ring Frankie had bought fitted perfectly and within seconds the whole restaurant was applauding them.

Even once the couple had become engaged the usual problems were still there – fitting Catherine in with Frankie's racing commitments. Finding a quiet date in the diary to get married would prove problematic. Frankie sat down with his Godolphin friend and colleague, Simon Crisford, to try to overcome this inevitable difficulty. After some time flicking through the pages of Frankie's diary, Simon found a suitable date. The wedding was fixed for Sunday, 20 July 1997.

The day before the wedding was to prove an eventful one. Frankie won two races at Newmarket that afternoon and managed to pick up a three-day suspension in the process, which, as luck would have it, would prove enough time to allow him a brief honeymoon with Catherine in the South of France some eight days after the wedding.

Frankie has never been afraid of breaking with convention and his stag night was to prove no exception. Evidently not one for superstition, he and his friends ended up in the same club as Catherine and her hen party, which evolved into a champagne fight between the contingents.

After a heavy night's drinking, Frankie retired to the Bedford Lodge Hotel, where he had been staying for the previous two months while his house was being renovated. He awoke on the day of the wedding the worse for wear, not helped by the massive fry-up he downed at breakfast.

Frankie and his best man, Colin Rate, decided to try and walk off his hangover and so set off down Newmarket High Street. When they returned to the hotel, Frankie was handed a fax which read, 'My congratulations to you both. Elizabeth R. ' Suddenly Frankie felt good again.

The wedding took place that afternoon at the Catholic church in Newmarket. The ceremony itself went more-or-less smoothly – there was a slight glitch when Catherine struggled to fit the ring onto Frankie's finger. They left the church to find at least 500 people waiting outside.

A lavish reception took place that evening. A ten-piece orchestra had been hired for the occasion, but Rolling Stone Ronnie Wood stole the show with his emotional rendition of 'Amazing Grace'. The newlyweds left the reception at around two in the morning and headed for their new home in Stretchworth. Frankie just managed to carry Catherine over the threshold before they both collapsed into bed and fell asleep with exhaustion.

The honeymoon allowed them to snatch a few rare and precious days together when Frankie could devote all his time to his wife without having to worry about being called away on riding duty.

And so began a down-to-earth, stable and low-key marriage which does not draw attention to itself, seek the limelight or feed scraps to gossip lovers. There is nothing to suggest theirs is anything other than a normal, happy marriage, which has undoubtedly made a massive contribution towards keeping Frankie on the straight and narrow, thus helping him remain focussed on riding and away from the temptations and distractions his fame and charisma inevitably bring.

Further happiness was to follow in 1999 with the birth of their first son, Leonardo. The previous day had been disappointing for Frankie as his horse, the beautiful grey Godolphin flagship Daylami, failed to win the Prix de l' Arc de Triomphe at Longchamp. This loss was to be put firmly into perspective that night when a heavily pregnant Catherine phoned Frankie worried that she could not feel the baby moving inside her.

Frankie flew straight home early the following

morning and took her to the hospital in Cambridge for a check-up. A decision was taken to induce the baby. After Catherine had been given the injection she and Frankie went for a short walk and Catherine began having spasms. After a mercifully short labour of around two hours, Leonardo was born. An unusually apprehensive Frankie was invited to cut the umbilical cord by the nurse, something he couldn't bring himself to manage. However, it wouldn't be long before the showman in Frankie returned.

He headed to the nearest off-licence, bought a bottle of champagne and returned to the hospital to share it with Catherine. Unsurprisingly Catherine wasn't up for a heavy drinking session and only managed half a glass or so whilst Frankie polished off the rest single-handed, before crashing out beside Catherine on her hospital bed, only to be awoken some time later by a sharp nudge to find his wife squashed uncomfortably into the corner of the bed whilst he'd taken most of the covers, snoring loudly. After this, Frankie was put firmly in his place – on the camp bed on the floor, where he spent the rest of the night.

And so Frankie's status as a family man through and through was confirmed. It wouldn't be long before Leo found himself a brother to Ella, Mia and Tallula. Without question, Frankie's conversion from party animal to devoted family man was complete.

CHAPTER 8

Getting Serious

Frankie returned from Morocco on New Year's Eve 1993 and paid a visit to John Gosden's home. John claimed he didn't recognise the new, shaven-headed, slimmed down, lean, tanned Frankie. They were ready for battle to commence on the all-weather tracks on New Year's Day.

The season got off to a dream start at Lingfield as Frankie won the first flat race of the year on Tiddy Oggie, and then turned it into a double in the next race.

Whilst most of his competitors were topping up their suntans in warmer climes, Frankie sat down with Mattie and prepared a rigorous schedule, which would see him riding on a daily basis at Lingfield, Wolverhampton and Southwell. He was so determined, that on Saturdays he would often start at Lingfield in the afternoon and then end the day with several more rides at Wolverhampton under the floodlights.

That said, if he thought he was going to have it all his own way over the next three months, he could think again. Jason Weaver was hungry for success and had shown a similar level of dedication. There were going to be some interesting battles ahead.

Frankie won a treble at Southwell on 7 January, and before the month was over he secured several more doubles at Lingfield and a four-timer at Wolverhampton.

By February, Frankie started riding out for John Gosden at Stanley House, showing a keenness and hunger to get to know each of the horses he had not seen since his early days with Luca.

The highlight of the all-weather season came on a day in early March, which began at Lingfield when Frankie won the opening race on Letsbehonestaboutit. He added a second victory with Spender, and was narrowly denied a third when Jason Weaver's horse, Plinth, edged past. Then it was straight in the car, around the M25, and up the M4 to Wolverhampton where Frankie arrived with just minutes to spare to ride Chairman's Choice in the opening race. The horse disappointed, but by the end of the evening Frankie had made it five winners in a day.

By the time the season proper began, Frankie had built up a firm lead in the jockey's championship, which would be his to lose from then on. The only realistic threat was surely going to come from Jason Weaver, who had applied himself in a similar way to

Frankie. By this point, Frankie and Jason's lead would be too far for the likes of Pat Eddery to beat.

Just as importantly, Frankie was a wiser jockey than he had been. In the past, if he found himself boxed in he would do everything he could to get out of it, putting the wellbeing of himself and the horse at enormous risk. But now he realised that he may have lost out on one race, but there would be plenty more races, on this and other days, and it was better to concede defeat in one particular race than to risk injury and be sidelined for weeks, giving others the chance to climb up the table. His experience on sand in America also helped his cause and gave him an enormous advantage over other jockeys.

Meanwhile, Sheikh Mohammed bin Rashid Al Maktoum was preparing the ground to make his stables dominant players in the global racing scene. His enthusiasm for both horse and camel racing was never in question. Joined by his senior wife, Sheikha Hind bint Maktoum bin Juma Al Maktoum, and his junior wife, Princess Haya bint Al-Hussein, both of whom share their husband's passion for racing, they set about their ambition using techniques that would revolutionise racing.

The Sheikh built a training base at Al Quoz, in the Dubai desert not far from the City of Dubai. Initially, it was fairly modest, consisting of a barn and a small number of horses. However, over a remarkably short period of time, the outfit quickly developed into the massive Godolphin unit. Al Quoz has capacity for 140 horses in state-of-the-art boxes, a private training track and an equine swimming pool.

This base was supported by the Dubai Equine Hospital, which gives unrivalled veterinary care to the Godolphin horses. Then there was the Dubai feed-mill, which, using a scientific approach, gives the Godolphin horses the best possible nourishment. No matter where they are in the world, Godolphin horses are always fed with the produce of the Dubai feed-mill. Nad al Sheba, home of the Dubai World Cup, is just a stone's throw away, and is where the majority of Godolphin horses are concentrated.

Their base in Britain is Stanley House in Newmarket, which has subsequently been renamed Godolphin Stables, situated on Bury Road, away from the main string of stables. Ironically, it is on the same road as Frankie's home when he first arrived in Newmarket. It is also situated right next to the Limekilns, the best grass gallops in Newmarket. Godolphin also uses another Newmarket yard, Moulton Paddocks. Nothing is left to chance, only the very best will do. The Sheikh has always been prepared to put his money where his mouth is to achieve his bold ambition.

Sheikh Mohammed is very much a hands-on boss, who plays an active part in the day-to-day running of the operation. He is known to take seriously the views of his trainers and jockeys, yet he remains fiercely independent, never afraid to disagree with anyone and take a bold or ambitious decision when he feels the need to.

His greatest brainwave to date has undoubtedly been his decision to winter all Godolphin horses in Dubai. This allows them to spend the winter months away from the bitter cold of Newmarket in favour of a more suitable climate. When they return to Newmarket in March their coats are in shiny, immaculate condition and they are at the peak of physical fitness for the start of the season. Time has proven the true significance and impact of this decision; but back in 1993, the racing public in Britain had not yet realised just how smart a move this was.

Frankie was to ride Balanchine for Godolphin in the 1,000 Guineas at Newmarket. Pre-season, Frankie and Ray Cochrane were recruited to ride in a searching Guineas trial at Nad al Sheba. Frankie and Balanchine finished second to State Performer. Following the race, Frankie spoke at length with the Sheikh about the horse's performance in the race. Despite a previously mixed reputation, Frankie was impressed with the horse's performance and told the Sheikh he thought the horse could well finish within the first three in the 1,000 Guineas.

The bookies, not realising the significance of wintering the horse in Dubai, begged to differ, and made Balanchine a 20-1 outsider. On the big day, Frankie and Balanchine only lost out to Las Meninas, ridden by John Reid and ironically owned by the late Robert Sangster, whom the Sheikh had bought Balanchine from just six months earlier.

Godolphin was still in its infancy, but on that day they had dealt a significant warning shot to the racing public that they meant business, and that wintering horses in Dubai certainly brought its rewards.

On the Saturday of the 2,000 Guineas, Frankie found

himself on Grand Lodge for Willie Jarvis, which it was thought stood a reasonable chance. Over the final furlong and a half, Frankie found himself locked in a tight duel with Mister Baileys, ridden by Jason Weaver, still very much his only realistic obstacle to becoming champion jockey.

It was too close to call as they crossed the line but the photo clearly showed Mister Baileys had won. Frankie's confidence suffered a cruel blow at the loss – he'd narrowly missed out on winning two Classics in a short space of time.

His confidence received a temporary lift when he won on Lochsong once again, this time in the Palace House Stakes, in spite of trainer Ian Balding's warning that she was only 80 per cent fit.

But they say bad luck comes in threes, and this was certainly to prove the case for Frankie at the Italian 2,000 Guineas the following day, when he again finished second, narrowly missing out riding Blinding Speed. His self-belief took a further blow, he had finished second in three Classics in the space of four days. He replayed every race in his head and wondered what he had to do to capture victory. Did he have what it takes to win a Classic? He was plagued by self-doubt and was in serious need of a lift.

It helped that the newly-retired Gianfranco had flown over to Newmarket for a few weeks to lift his son's spirits. Another positive development was that his relationship with John Gosden was markedly different to the one he had had with Luca Cumani. Although it was true that Frankie was now a very different person to the irresponsible teenager who has worked for Luca, in John he had a boss who was a father figure, a confidant and a friend, someone who was well and truly on his side.

He confided in John, on a flight to France in May, that he was on the verge of burnout. He had been riding flat out since the start of the year, living on a diet of fresh air, and it was taking its toll. John took Frankie's concerns seriously – he knew he wasn't playing up and allowed him a few days off to catch up with sleep and recharge his batteries.

By June, Frankie had a golden opportunity to win his first Classic, riding Balanchine once again. He felt confident the horse was better suited to stepping up to a mile and a half after his experience in the 1,000 Guineas earlier in the season. Yet it was a happy accident that largely contributed to Frankie's success in this race.

Many jockeys choose to wear light, nylon gloves to give them a firm grip of the reins. Frankie thought he'd made a serious mistake when he left his in the weighing room. It turned out to be a blessing in disguise. Balanchine leaped out of the stalls, pulling fiercely, leaving the reins to slide straight through Frankie's hands. This left him with no choice but to let her run as fast as she liked and hope she held out to win. Everything now depended on Frankie's theory that the horse was best suited to a mile and a half being true.

All he could do now to aid his cause was to glide Balanchine towards the ground on the stands side at

Epsom, the best place to be in wet weather. As the race progressed, the only real opposition came from Walter Swinburn on Hawajiss. By the final hundred yards, Frankie had built up an unassailable lead, despite having very few ways of controlling the horse. His first British Classic victory was finally in the bag, much to his excitement and, no doubt, relief, after the agony he had endured earlier in the season.

The day before Royal Ascot, Luca contacted Frankie and booked him for his filly Relatively Special in the Coronation Stakes. Clearly Luca didn't feel the need to carry out his threat not to hire Frankie's services for a year. He'd seen enough to be convinced that Frankie was a changed man and was keen to make the most of someone who was likely to be crowned champion jockey before long. Relatively Special disappointed in the race, but it was a massive relief for Frankie to have finally ended his feud with Luca, to whom he undoubtedly owes a great deal for his development as a jockey, despite their uneasy relationship. Frankie would go on to ride plenty more winners for Luca in the years ahead, the most memorable being Falbrav in Hong Kong in December 2003.

The highlight of Royal Ascot for Frankie was riding Lochsong to a commanding victory in the Stand Stakes. The six-year-old could do no wrong that year and played no small part in lifting Frankie's confidence when it was most needed.

Frankie found himself back on Balanchine in an attempt to win a Classic double in the Irish Derby. This time Frankie remembered his gloves and felt he stood every chance of winning. She began pulling after three furlongs, but Frankie was in a position to skilfully manoeuvre her when the chance arose. She took the lead with half a mile to run, and Frankie let her accelerate early in the straight, and notched up a famous Classic double.

Balanchine ran in the colours of Sheikh Mohammed's brother, Sheikh Maktoum, but Frankie found himself greeted by an excitable Sheikh Mohammed after the race, holding Frankie's hand up in triumph as they passed the main stand. Godolphin was making its presence felt, and the Sheikh's efforts were starting to pay off in a major way.

Unfortunately, Balanchine was never given the opportunity to maximise her potential. The Irish Derby was to be her last race. Just three weeks later she nearly died from an attack of colic. Whilst the highly-skilled vets managed to save her, it was clear her racing days were over. This came as a massive blow to everyone involved with Godolphin, not least the Sheikh himself.

As is often the case with people, truly great horses tend to have imbalanced personalities. This certainly proved to be the case with Lochsong as the season progressed. Never an easy character, her wilder side surfaced on the day of the July Cup at Newmarket. Frankie was claimed to ride Catrail for Godolphin, so it was left to Willie Carson to ride the great Lochsong.

Her chance was lost before the race even started as she rushed down to the start far too quickly, with Willie unable to control her. This could, perhaps, be put down to Willie not being used to the horse, and indeed that seemed to be the case, as when Frankie was back on board in the King George V Stakes at Goodwood she won in convincing style in the pouring rain. But, as Frankie would soon discover, all was not well with his beloved Lochsong.

On the day of the Nunthorpe Stakes at York, Lochsong was the odds-on favourite, but Frankie didn't share the bookies' optimism. The horse became agitated on the way to the saddling boxes, tossing her head restlessly in anticipation of the battle ahead. And Frankie found her impossible to control as they made their way to the start. She wanted to be in control of things and wasn't going to let Frankie guide her in any way. She charged as quickly as she could, leaving Frankie completely powerless to do anything about it. Despite having a few minutes to relax when they reached the stalls, Lochsong was burnt out and there was nowhere near enough time for her to recover before the race began. She shot out and dominated the first furlong, but the entire field had overtaken them by the halfway stage, leaving Lochsong and Frankie stumbling in last, and many a punter severely out of pocket.

Lochsong's season may have been going off the rails somewhat, but Frankie's certainly wasn't. Two days later, Frankie rode his one-thousandth ride of the year on Osato at Ripon. And he got off to a blistering start in September as he rode a treble at York, landing him the fastest double-century at the same time.

Frankie's next encounter with Lochsong was fast approaching and it was to come at Longchamp. By now Ian Balding was as worried as Frankie about Lochsong's temperament. Ian tried to appease this by getting permission from the stewards to leave the paddock fifteen minutes early, allowing Frankie to walk her to the start accompanied by strong men on either side and at the point where she would emerge onto the course. This was done to have every angle covered and to avoid a repeat of her last outing.

This course of action was probably the right one, as although Lochsong was as restless as before, at least they arrived at the start in one piece. In a way, Frankie had done the hardest part. The race got off to a superb start, bringing out all of Lochsong's best qualities, leaving Frankie with very little work to do. However, there was always the chance something could go horribly wrong, and Frankie wasn't taking anything for granted until they had passed the winning post. However, they had built up a commanding lead early on which secured them victory in the Prix de l'Abbaye de Longchamp for the second year in a row. Owner Jeff Smith had certainly got his money's worth out of Lochsong, whose career earnings had overtaken the £600,000 mark with this spectacular victory.

By this time Frankie's hectic schedule was taking its toll and he decided that with such a big lead over Jason Weaver in the table he could afford to take a short break. John Gosden advised Frankie not to burn himself out during the final weeks of the season – he had done more than enough for him, and the title of Champion Jockey was safely in the bag.

However, there was one more record that Frankie wanted to break before the 1994 season came to a close.

Gianfranco had achieved 229 wins in Italy in 1983, and Frankie wanted to overtake that number in Britain. He managed it, bringing the season's tally to 233 before taking a well-earned rest, winding down a few weeks before the season came to a close in late October.

Late in the year Frankie headed to Churchill Downs to take part in the Breeders' Cup, which was to be Lochsong's final race. As restless as ever, she managed to clock up the final three furlongs in 33.1 seconds three days prior to the Sprint.

By this stage, there was probably very little point in trying to form a race plan for Lochsong, but Frankie and Ian's idea was to take the bend at a strong canter before letting her stride on the straight at half pace. However, as this was Lochsong, all concerned could only predict the unpredictable. For the first time ever, she wasn't keen to jump out of the stalls, and she didn't seem enthusiastic about racing. Once out, she began to charge and there was nothing Frankie could do, but she soon tired and the race was lost. Frankie eased up, and Lochsong came in fourteenth and last place.

Nobody could work out what went wrong. Lochsong was a lot of things, but she was not a quitter and her lack of enthusiasm had taken everyone by surprise. Subsequent X-rays showed she had chipped a bone in one of her knees, which probably occurred during the strenuous work-out three days before.

It was a sad end to a great career, but Lochsong is still remembered as the people's favourite and is surely one of the finest horses Frankie has ever ridden. She is perhaps the greatest horse of all time over five furlongs.

GETTING SERIOUS

The trip to Churchill Downs was far from a wasted one for Frankie, in spite of the bitter disappointment Lochsong had brought him. He finished fourth on Belle Genius for Paul Kelleway in the Juvenile. In the Mile, Frankie rode Barathea for Luca, who he had been testing over an American bend on the gallops at Newmarket. He had told Luca he felt the horse was in great shape and could cope very well with Churchill Downs.

Frankie put his plan into action with perfection. He started the race placing himself just behind the leaders. Barathea cruised into the bend, the only horse in the race still on the bridle. Frankie let him go in the final furlong, with plenty still in the tank allowing him to charge to a superb victory.

Then came the moment Frankie had waited nine years for. He had been practicing Angel Cordero's flying dismount for the previous nine years, and finally unleashed it after this victory. Luca was terrified Frankie would break his leg, but nothing was going to change his mind. His heart was set on it and there was nowhere better for him to try it out than in Angel's own back yard. It may be hard to imagine now, but at the time Frankie's flying dismount faced a barrage of criticism in the British media. Letters flooded in to the racing papers, condemning him as un-gentlemanly and very un-British. In later years the flying dismount would become one of Frankie's much-loved trademarks.

As 1994 came to a close, Frankie's hard work had certainly paid off. The controversies of eighteen months earlier were a distant memory, even in the minds of those he'd hurt the most, such as Luca. Frankie was Champion Jockey, and had ridden a total of 244 winners around the world, 233 of which came on British soil, the highest number of winners since Gordon Richards scored 261 in 1949, under very different circumstances. Frankie rode in a record-breaking 1318 races in Britain that year, a statistic that illustrates the level of dedication he had to riding. The hard work and the sacrifices had well and truly paid off.

CHAPTER 9

Hitting the Big Time

Frankie spent the winter that followed his triumphant season in much the same way as he had the previous year – in Morocco with his father under a strict regime of diet and exercise. He returned to Britain in time for the start of the all-weather programme on 2 January. He was as hungry as before to retain the title and knew there was still a great deal to prove. Some still doubted the extent of his talent, believing him to be a one-year wonder, while others still held the view that a return to his wild ways wasn't too far away.

Also hungry for success was Frankie's arch-rival the previous season, Jason Weaver, who would be taking the all-weather winter calendar just as seriously as before – if not more so. Jason had shown signs of incredible ambition towards the end of the previous season, even when he knew Frankie's lead over him in the table was too great. He followed in Frankie's footsteps and recorded a double-century for the year. Only five people had done it before, now two had done it in one year. Jason had fired a warning shot firmly in Frankie's direction.

Frankie got off to a superb start in 1995, riding seven winners in three days, starting at Southwell on 2 January. But Jason was just as keen, and matched Frankie stride for stride. Retaining the title of Champion Jockey was going to be a long, hard battle. As with the previous season, there were only going to be two contenders, the other big names clearly, either, hadn't learnt a lesson from the previous season, or were not willing to sacrifice a large chunk of their winter breaks in the name of gaining the title. But this one rival was too serious for Frankie, and it was clear he wasn't going to be able to trounce him in the table the way he had done the previous year.

Their relationship became increasingly strained over the early months of the season. They had been firm friends for many years, both being pupils of Luca's. Until now they had travelled to meetings together and been quick to pat each other on the back after winning races. This all changed. There was no room for such a friendship when their rivalry was so fierce.

Frankie found it easy to get on with Jason when he was top of the table. Now that Jason was ahead, Frankie was less willing to be friendly. It is rare for anyone to see an unpleasant side to Frankie's character. He can be moody, but not nasty. Jason was to be the exception. His only crime was being a threat to Frankie's dominance, but it was one Frankie struggled to cope with in a gentlemanly way.

The bitterness between them came to a head at Lingfield on 16 March. As was often the case, Frankie and Jason were the only serious contenders, with Frankie riding the favourite, Nordico Express, and Jason on Dolly Face. Frankie made the early running but Jason made a late charge with two furlongs left.

They fought like the prize on offer was the Derby rather than a minor race in front of just a handful of people. In the end, Jason stole the race and let off steam in the moments that followed. He turned to Frankie offering a high five, but Frankie responded with a tirade of insults. It was a sign of things to come for the following eight months.

April saw Frankie being voted Jockey of the Year, and Flat Jockey of the Year, at Lester's annual awards dinner. It was confirmation by all involved in the racing industry that Frankie was now a major player and a very real threat to racing's old guard.

Godolphin was, by this time, an increasingly well-oiled machine, a position which was enhanced still further with the appointment of Saeed bin Suroor as trainer. A former policeman, Saeed had taken out his licence just a year previously and was now spending half his year in Al Quoz and the other half in Newmarket – a lucrative position he remains in to this day, and he soon built a warm friendship and close professional relationship with Frankie.

The appointment quickly brought rewards to Godolphin, as Frankie rode Vettori to victory in the

French 2,000 Guineas at Longchamp. Shortly afterwards, Frankie rode another of Saeed's horses, Moonshell to third place in the 1,000 Guineas, which taught him a lot about the horse and led him to conclude that the best was yet to come.

Frankie was back on board Moonshell in the Oaks at Epsom. They took the lead after two furlongs and there was never any doubt that the race was in the bag, despite a late charge from Walter Swinburn on Dance a Dream.

Derby day was, as usual, a disappointing one for Frankie. Sheikh Mohammed would probably have put Frankie on Lammtarra given the choice, and he may well have been given the ride were it not for the fact he was retained to ride the Sheikh's horses trained by John Gosden, which resulted in Frankie being given Tamure, who stood a realistic chance of victory having won his previous three races. Walter was the lucky man who got to ride Lammtarra and it proved an ideal opportunity to get his revenge on Frankie for the Oaks defeat.

The build-up to the race for Lammtarra had been far from ideal. Some months before, he had suffered a blood disorder that nearly killed him and kept him out of training. Sheikh Mohammed visited Lammtarra every day in Al Quoz that winter to monitor his progress, holding an instinctive faith in a horse most people considered a no-hoper for the Derby, having ridden just once before and come down with a very serious illness shortly afterwards.

Frankie began the race well, and things were going to plan until Tamure took too long to overtake the leader,

Fahal. When he finally succeeded, Frankie thought he had done enough to win, before a late surge from Walter on Lammtarra twenty yards from home stole the race. Frankie found this cruel defeat hard to take, but he was far more courteous with Walter than with Jason, joining him and the Godolphin team for a celebratory Chinese meal in Newmarket that evening.

The following Monday it was back to the day-to-day business of trying to trounce Jason. By now, Frankie had a slender lead over him in the table, but there was still a great deal of work to be done. Frankie rode his hundredth winner of the season on Persian Secret and was well on course for a double century for the second successive season.

By early July, Frankie was presented with a choice of two horses to ride in the Coral-Eclipse Stakes at Sandown – both were trained by John Gosden for Godolphin. Having seen them working together at the stables, Frankie favoured Halling over Red Bishop. However, his was a minority opinion and others tried to persuade him that Red Bishop, who had ridden all over the world, was the best horse available to him. He should have gone with his instincts. In the end, he chose Red Bishop, and Walter mounted Halling. It turned out to be a huge mistake. Halling made the running and the only horse that threatened him throughout the race was Singspiel, but Halling hung on for victory, leaving Frankie trailing way back. The bad choice of horse was made worse by the fact that first place was worth £150,000.

During a suspension later that month, Frankie

headed for a short break at Gianfranco's home in Sardinia. During a lazy day on the beach, an excitable Mattie rang with some fantastic news for Frankie. He had been booked to ride Lammtarra in the King George VI and Queen Elizabeth Diamond Stakes at Ascot later that week. Frankie was understandably taken aback by this, as it was assumed Walter would be riding him again, but it turned out Walter had had a row with certain quarters, leaving the coast clear for Frankie. He was naturally delighted, but could expect a rough ride from the press in the days leading up to the race.

The papers took Walter's side, even though the full facts about the row which led to his removal have never come to light. Nevertheless, this increased the pressure on Frankie and he was aware he had a lot to prove. A long chat with Walter helped Frankie get a feel for the horse, which helped enormously since he'd never ridden him before, but this would be a massive first test nonetheless.

In the closing stages of the race, Frankie didn't have it all his own way. Lammtarra didn't react to Frankie's methods of encouragement. On the straight, Michael Hills on Pentire sped past. Only then did Lammtarra rise to the challenge and the pair ran neck and neck in the last few furlongs. As the final stages approached, though, Pentire was burnt out, leaving Frankie enough time to regain the lead and hold on for victory.

Sheikh Mohammed made little effort to hide his excitement at the end of that race, and maintains that was the finest ride Frankie had ever given a Godolphin horse, but even Frankie was taken aback by how

Lammtarra responded to the late challenge, and put the victory down to the horse's endeavours rather than his own.

In August, Frankie was due to ride Wainwright, one of his favourite horses, at Haydock. It was to be the horse's final race before retirement, and since he had terrible feet, the Sheikh had agreed to let Frankie have the horse as a pet for Catherine. However, it wasn't to be.

During the race, Frankie sustained a terrible fall when Wainwright snapped one of his forelegs. The horse had to be put down and Frankie was knocked out cold for several minutes after he came crashing to the ground head first. He was lucky to be alive, and even luckier to be able to ride at York two weeks later. Fortunately he was discharged from hospital the following day and with the help of masseur Andrew Ferguson made it to York, but this fall was one of the worst of his career and could have been much, much worse.

As Frankie's first race approached at the York meeting, he was nervous. The fall had taken its toll and he worried about how well he was able to perform. Luckily he was able to silence his own criticism as he rode to victory on So Factual.

Another historic landmark came in September, when he rode his thousandth winner. It came at Doncaster on 9 September on Classic Cliché for Godolphin in the St Leger. He was extra keen to seal this race due to the tradition of awarding a velvet cap to the winner, which gained extra significance with him reaching such a milestone in the race. He celebrated with champagne all round for the jockeys present.

By the time October came round Frankie's main focus was the Arc. It was the race that had excited him the most as he was growing up in Italy, with its rich array of jockeys and horses from Britain, France and Italy. When discussing the race in the office, Frankie told Simon Crisford he would prefer to ride Balanchine over Lammtarra, a view formed when he rode Balanchine in the Prix Foy in September and had only just been beaten by the previous year's Arc winner Carnegie.

However, the Sheikh had other ideas. Simon picked up the phone to call him and told him of Frankie's preference. The Sheikh was having none of it, and told Simon that Frankie was riding Lammtarra before putting the phone down.

Gianfranco had spent the preceding weeks telling his son how important it was to make a fast start in the Arc, based on his own wealth of experience of riding in the race. In his mind, the most important thing was to get in the first three early on. Frankie knew he was right.

It would be only the fourth race Lammtarra had been in, but as the son of Nijinsky out of the Oaks winner Snow Bride, he was bred to be a success and the Sheikh's decision looked like being a logical one.

Frankie put the race plan into action, settling him into second place, around four lengths behind the leader, Luso. He decided to begin his charge at the top of the straight, and it wasn't long before Lammtarra eased past Luso. A late challenge from Olivier Peslier on Freedom Cry from the middle was the only real threat posed, but

Lammtarra found some extra pace in the closing moments of the race to hold on for a famous victory.

Frankie was on cloud nine following this victory. He gave an extra-enthusiastic flying dismount, before being embraced by the Sheikh. This was one of the proudest days of Frankie's career, one never to be forgotten. For Godolphin, too, it was an important milestone in the team's development. On the plane journey home, they held a champagne celebration with Frankie still full of energy and completely out of control after sealing victory in the race he'd wanted to win for so long.

He was brought back down to earth at Pontefract the next day when he was slapped with a lengthy ban under the new totting up procedure. He was found guilty of irresponsible riding on the exotically-named La Alla Wa Asa, but Frankie felt he'd been treated harshly by the stewards and claimed the horse's inexperience was responsible for taking somebody out.

However, there wasn't time to dwell on this, as two days later he rode a treble at York, which notched up his two-hundredth winner of the season on Sheer Danzig, making Frankie the first jockey since Sir Gordon Richards in 1952 to ride back-to-back double centuries.

The following month Frankie was crowned champion jockey once again, with 216 winners, fewer than the previous year but still mighty impressive when considering the higher number of injuries and suspensions.

That winter would see a change in routine from the previous two years. The rules were changing and winners on the all-weather circuit would no longer count towards the title. Even if this hadn't been the case, it would almost certainly have seen a change in emphasis for Frankie due to Godolphin's rapidly expanding global commitments, which saw Frankie riding all over the world on a more regular basis.

At the start of the 1996 season, Frankie's contract was changed. John Gosden would no longer have first claim on his services. That honour would now go to Godolphin. Then came the Sheikh's horses with other trainers in Britain and France. Under the terms of the contract, Frankie was being paid a considerable sum as a retainer. A sign of his increasing prosperity was the Mercedes car, which he regularly replaced.

In sharp contrast to the previous two winters, in 1996 Frankie found himself in Al Quoz, riding Godolphin's horses most mornings at sunrise before it became unbearably hot by mid morning.

Never one to sit back and relax, the Sheikh continued to expand his racing empire, announcing that the first Dubai World Cup was to take place at Nad Al Sheba on 27 March, with a £1.5 million first prize. This was enough to tempt the top American dirt specialists to make the journey to Dubai. The build-up to the race was unparalleled, and included a lavish beach party attended by thousands of guests, including an array of catwalk and movie stars. Later in the week there was a private concert given by Mick Hucknell and Simply Red. Nothing on this scale had ever been seen before anywhere in the racing world.

Godolphin stood a good chance in the race with four

runners in total, with Frankie riding Halling. However, they were always going to be up against it as the American horses were far more used to the dirt tracks, and a horse being able to make a sound transition from track to dirt could never be taken for granted.

Halling had a poor draw on the inside close to the rails, which was a further disadvantage. In the end, the only contenders in the race were the three American horses. The highest placed European horse was Pentire, in fourth. It was clear Godolphin still had a great deal of learning to do on dirt.

Back in Britain, Godolphin's fortunes improved as the flat season got underway. Frankie won the 2,000 Guineas in a thrilling race on Mark Of Esteem. But he found it hard to judge the horse's character having only seen him in recent races. He led Mark Of Esteem into the lead earlier than he should have, and ended up in a three-horse battle with Philip Robinson on Even Top and Jason Weaver on Bijou d'Inde. As they crossed the line no one was sure which of the three had won, least of all Frankie who was cursing himself for having moved too soon.

The three horses were made to wait and circle as the photo was examined. There was only around an inch in it. Fortunately for Frankie, he had done enough and his number was duly called out. He was ecstatic and went into one of his uncontrollably high moods, leaping into the air and landing in the arms of travelling head lad John Davis. He had won the race his father had twice triumphed in during the seventies, and following in his footsteps evidently meant a lot to him. But he would soon be brought back down to earth.

Frankie had made illegal contact with John prior to weighing in, which resulted in a £500 fine. Worse was to follow when all three jockeys involved in the battle were suspended for illegal use of the whip. Jason got two days, Philip got four, and Frankie was given an especially harsh eight-day ban.

The following day Frankie received a barrage of negative publicity from the press – his actions were condemned as cruel and were compared to that of an outdated circus act. In truth, this was not entirely accurate. Frankie was seen whipping the horse quickly and in quick succession. The strength of the contact would not have been anywhere near as severe as if he had struck him full force less frequently.

Luckily the bad press generated from the 2,000 Guineas didn't stick, and Frankie soon found himself doing publicity work for the Vodafone Derby, which was in the process of going through a radical change of image as it moved from its traditional timeslot of the first Wednesday in June to the nearest Saturday. With Frankie very much the fresh young face of modern racing, he was seen as the ideal ambassador by Epsom racecourse.

Another leading sportsman who was signed up by Vodafone for publicity purposes was Vinnie Jones, who quickly struck up an enduring friendship with Frankie that would lead to Vinnie being represented by Frankie's manager Peter Burrell. However, Vinnie wasn't going to excuse Frankie from his renowned hell-raising tactics. On a trip to Epsom with his old team-mates from Wimbledon FC, Vinnie decided Frankie needed to be punished for tipping them a loser. Frankie had told them before racing that the ironically-named Selhurstparkflyer was going to win. But come the race Frankie beat them on the line on Lord Oliver. At the end of the day, Frankie went to join the boys for a drink. Vinnie and co took their revenge by hanging Frankie upside down by his ankles fifty feet above the ground and threatened to drop him if he ever tipped them another loser!

Frankie never really stood a chance in the 1996 Derby. Godolphin didn't have a serious contender, so Frankie was free to ride the John Gosden-trained colt Shantou, owned by the Sheikh. Shantou struggled with the pace, and coming down the hill was way back, but ended up in a rugged battle with Pat Eddery on Dushyantor. Their battle gained momentum and eventually Dushyantor finished second with Frankie close behind on Shantou, in a Derby won convincingly by Michael Hills on Shaamit.

The Epsom meeting wasn't an entirely disappointing one for Frankie, as he secured victory in the Coronation Cup on Swain in a riveting finish with Michael Kinane riding Singspiel. This was Frankie's first ride for Andre Fabre, who instructed Frankie to make a quick start, ease off at the top of the hill and then charge down for the finish. For once, Frankie did as he was told, and secured a thrilling victory against another truly great horse.

The season was going from strength to strength and hit its zenith on 12 June when Frankie rode a treble at

Yarmouth. He then took to the skies before arriving at Kempton where he rode another treble at the evening meeting. As is often the case throughout Frankie's career, something would bring him back down to earth before very long, and the following day at Newbury that happened in horrific style.

Frankie was to ride the grey, Shawanni, for Godolphin in the Ballymacoll Stakes that day, an unpredictable, fierce and stubborn horse who was difficult for anybody to control. Frankie had ridden her in the French 1,000 Guineas where she seemed out of control for large sections of the race.

On this occasion, as Frankie went to mount the filly before the race the omens were not good. She didn't move once Frankie got on board and it took an enormous effort to get her going. He asked her lad to turn her behind some of the other horses in an attempt to get her to relax. It didn't work.

She took just a few steps before coming to a halt once again. The next time she showed signs of movement she threw Frankie to the ground, rearing backwards on top of him. He crashed down onto the tarmac below with an almighty thud. This was going to be a serious one.

The medical team present were initially unable to appreciate the full extent of his injuries, and believed all he was suffering from was some bruising. But Frankie knew things were far worse; he was convinced he'd done severe damage to his elbow. He was taken by ambulance to the Royal Berkshire Hospital and made to wait an hour and a half in a lengthy queue before he was taken in for X-rays.

It turned out Frankie's prognosis was spot on and the bone from his upper arm had been forced right through the elbow joint. Fortunately for Frankie, the consultant was free to operate the following morning, but a lengthy period of recuperation was inevitable and he was told he would be lucky to be back riding again before the end of the season.

What followed was a frustrating period when all Frankie could do was sit and do nothing. He put his feet up and watched Royal Ascot from home, seeing many horses win that he would have mounted had he been fit, including Classic Cliché in the Gold Cup. Matters weren't helped by Italy being knocked out of Euro '96 in the early stages. Tired of sitting around one day, Frankie borrowed a morning suit from Bruce Raymond and headed to Royal Ascot on Friday, where he got chatting to Ronnie Wood. The Rolling Stone turned out to be a huge racing enthusiast and would go on to play guitar at Frankie's wedding reception.

With time on his hands, Frankie relieved his boredom by heading to Gianfranco's apartment in Gran Canaria for a break with Catherine. Eager to get back riding as quickly as possible, he spent the first few days doing gentle exercises with his arm in the toddler's pool. Within a week he was swimming properly and quickly progressed to swimming in the sea with Gianfranco.

Frankie found ways to take his mind off the frustration and boredom of being out of action at the height of the season, but his mood wasn't helped when he found out on teletext that Halling, who had become a favourite ride of his, had won the Eclipse Stakes. He responded by heading straight for the pool and completing twenty-five laps in record time.

He returned home to see his specialist, convinced that the time had come to return to the saddle. The specialist shattered his hopes of a speedy return, since the bones in his elbow were not completely healed. There was more time to kill, so Frankie and Catherine headed to the sun once more, this time in Sardinia.

During this time, Frankie was the subject of a feature during the BBC's coverage of Glorious Goodwood. He rode out for Sussex trainer Lady Anne Heaves to help the BBC's racing presenter at the time, Julian Wilson, put together a piece on his recovery.

After the ride, Frankie sat down to breakfast next to Lady Anne's husband, Colin, where they were joined by Julian. The conversation between Julian and Colin quickly turned to cricket. Frankie was well aware that Julian was a massive cricket enthusiast, but having grown up in Italy, he had never managed to get to grips with the game. Julian started gibbering on about his exploits as a spin bowler for the Newmarket Trainers' XI, when he turned to Frankie and asked him if he was a fan. Frankie's response was blunt, as he told Julian in no uncertain terms that he found cricket the most boring sport on earth and couldn't understand why so many apparently sane people followed it.

Colin burst into fits of laughter as Julian gave Frankie the look of death, as though he'd just committed a cardinal sin. Julian then informed Frankie that Colin was, in fact, Sir Colin Cowdrey, a true cricketing legend and former England captain. Luckily for Frankie, the late Sir Colin saw the funny side of him making such a fool of himself, and then, in an attempt to improve Frankie's appreciation of the game, took him outside for some bowling lessons. It didn't really work, but Frankie and Sir Colin soon developed a firm friendship.

Incredibly, Frankie managed to beat the odds and return to riding on 9 August at Newmarket. However, his comeback would be marred by controversy, when the following week whilst riding at Windsor he finished third on Cape Pigeon. The horse was eleven by now and had become stubborn and set in his ways. During the early stages of the race he had battled for the lead with another horse but had quickly tired and was unable to finish higher than third.

A stewards' inquiry was held and Frankie's explanation that he had burnt his horse out by going too fast too soon was accepted. However, the horse's owner, the construction tycoon Eric Gadsden, wasn't so forgiving. He condemned Frankie's performance on the horse, saying, 'I don't think that Frankie tried very hard. I think the Jockey Club are very easily satisfied. They might consider viewing a video of the race. In the latter stages Frankie's upper-body movement was virtually non-existent –if the horse was tired why did he suddenly galvanise him into action when the second went past in the last 100 yards?'

These remarks were plastered all over the following day's papers. And worse still was to follow, when the horse's trainer Gerald Cottrell sided with Mr Gadsden, saying, 'I think Mr Gadsden has a point. I think he gave the horse a tender ride over the last two furlongs – he didn't look hard pushed to me. To put it mildly, he gave it a tender ride.'

This sort of publicity was the last thing Frankie needed. By his own admission, the ride wasn't his finest hour, but he was far from back to full fitness, and the horse's age and character counted against him. Claims he gave the horse a tender ride are very unfair, especially as the Jockey Club ruled this out but, as with most jockeys, Frankie's confidence is fragile and this caused a severe dent. A chat with John Gosden helped lift Frankie's mood a little. John told him to be natural and not to force anything. On 16 August, Frankie was back to his winning ways, picking up a treble at Newbury followed by a double on 17 August.

He was on a roll, and it continued the following day at Deauville when he secured the Prix Morny, riding Bahamian Bounty for David Loder. Then at York came a magnificent victory on Halling in the Juddmonte International. Again, this run of good fortune was not to last long. Frankie was still not one hundred per cent, and certainly not up to the level required for a gruelling three day meeting at York.

His relationship with fellow jockey Richard Quinn has never been an easy one. From time to time things have boiled over, and there have been many serious rows between them.

In the Yorkshire Oaks, Richard was riding Whitewater Affair whilst Frankie was on Russian Snows. As Richard's horse weakened, Frankie tried to pull through and the two horses touched. Unfortunately the cameras picked up on this and Frankie was banned for four days on grounds of irresponsible riding. Far worse clashes regularly occur and are barely noticed, but the head-on camera made this particular incident look especially bad and Frankie paid heavily for it.

Worse was to follow the next day. Frankie was in a hurry to lose weight so he could ride North Song for John Gosden, and was struggling to meet the 8st 6lb limit. He spent that morning running round the track and spent an unhealthy amount of time in the sauna. He rode in the first three races, but felt severely drained and was perspiring alarmingly.

He left the paddock on North Song and rode a mischievous race before finishing second. When Frankie tried to pull him up he went on a charge towards the starter's car. Frankie feared for his life – this was going to be serious. When a horse goes as wild as North Song there is nothing he, or anybody else can do to control him. However, suddenly, for no apparent reason, the horse just stopped. Frankie breathed a huge sigh of relief and headed for the unsaddling enclosure, where John was waiting to give him a lecture on his poor ride.

Frankie was in a zombie-like state as he somehow managed two more rides that afternoon. He wasn't well, and he knew it. After that final ride he was taken to the ambulance room and given Coca-Cola and tea saturated with sugar in an attempt to increase his energy levels. Frankie had gone too far. He had crossed the line between strict dieting and exercise, and over-doing it to dangerous proportions.

He was back in the saddle two days later though,

winning the Celebration Mile at Goodwood on that old favourite Mark Of Esteem. Meanwhile, the St Leger was fast approaching.

Frankie rode Shantou for John Gosden and ended up in a tussle with Pat Eddery on Dushyantor just as at Epsom earlier in the summer. Dushyantor held a firm lead until the final two furlongs, when the two were neck-and-neck and slogging it out for supremacy. Frankie guided Shantou into the centre of the course and, aided by some enthusiastic whipping, gained the lead with just a few strides left.

It was an emotional victory for Frankie as John had been taking a huge amount of stick in the press for his lack of success in the Classics. Frankie owed so much to John for keeping faith with him when he had gone off the rails a few short years earlier, and was especially glad to have brought him victory in a Classic. John had silenced Frankie's critics, now Frankie had returned the favour by managing to shut up all those who had questioned John's ability as a trainer in the lead-up to the race.

But, as usual, there was to be something round the corner to bring Frankie back down to earth. Both Frankie and Pat were suspended for illegal use of the whip in the final stages of the race. For Pat, this resulted in a two day ban, and Frankie got four, earning him the dubious honour of being the first jockey in history to collect separate whip bans in winning two Classics in the same year. A lengthy ban now seemed inevitable under racing's totting up procedure.

But there was no time to dwell on this. Frankie's life was about to change forever.

CHAPTER 10

The Magnificent Seven

On paper, it looked like being just another Saturday. Mary Bolton and her husband John made the journey from Somerset to London to celebrate their nineteenth wedding anniversary. John, a humble cattle dealer, was planning to go to Ascot for the day while his wife treated herself to a modest shopping spree.

Darren Yates was the owner of a struggling joinery business in Morecambe, Lancashire, making £300 on a good week. Times were hard; he worried constantly whether he'd have to lay off his six staff and was never sure whether he'd still be in business by Christmas. But this Saturday was a chance to take his mind off things with the usual Saturday routine, playing centre-half for his local football team, followed by a few pints in the pub.

For on-course bookmaker Gary Wiltshire times were more prosperous, life was comfortable. A standard Saturday was planned, working at Ascot during the day and Milton Keynes greyhounds in the evening.

On that day, Frankie wasn't in the best of moods, since the previous afternoon at Haydock had been completely unfruitful. That said, he usually enjoyed visiting Ascot for the Festival of British Racing Meeting, and he felt he had a good chance of winning on Wall Street in the first race. He also thought that Mark Of Esteem stood a decent chance in the third.

On this day, all of their lives would change forever, and for racing's profile, nothing would ever be the same again.

John Bolton decided to give his wife a minor interest in the day's racing. Mary, a fan of Frankie's charismatic qualities, asked her husband to put on a permutation of Frankie's mounts. John headed for Ladbrokes in Dover Street, Mayfair, where he decided to splash out more than usual. John bet on twenty-one £9 doubles, and a £5 each way accumulator, laying out a total of £216.91, including betting tax.

Darren Yates was made to promise his wife he would end his compulsive habit of backing Dettori. He reluctantly agreed, though sneakily staked £67.58 in his local William Hill shop in combining all seven of Dettori's mounts.

Frankie knew Wall Street had plenty of Stamina, and at 2-1 the bookies knew he stood a good chance in the Cumberland Lodge Stakes, his only real threat being Salmon Ladder. It wasn't long before Wall Street was out in front, and she was only really threatened by Salmon Ladder over the final few furlongs. In the end Wall Street pulled ahead and won by half a length.

The second race, the Diadem Stakes, saw Frankie ride Diffident, who he was convinced had no chance, and the starting price of 12-1 was, if anything, meanly priced. Frankie placed Diffident in behind the leading bunch, led by Averti, who led with a smart gallop. The horse in front was blocking Frankie's path, weaving sadistically from side to side, obstructing Frankie to the left, and then to the right. Time was running out. Frankie eventually managed to outsmart the turbulent horse and squeezed through on the left. Diffident managed to get his head in front of Leap For Joy, only for Lucayan Prince to join them, leaving little to choose as the trio of horses crossed the line. The photo confirmed that Diffident had stolen it by a short head from Lucayan Prince, with Leap For Joy another short head away in third.

Mary Bolton watched the first two races at the Holiday Inn in Mayfair, before heading off on her long-awaited shopping trip. Surely there was no point sacrificing her shopping for the faint possibility that Frankie might win the following five races, was there?

The third race was to be the most political of the day, with Frankie riding Mark of Esteem in the Queen Elizabeth II Stakes. There was certainly tension in the air for this one. Henry Cecil had trained the horse as a two-year-old and had fallen out with Sheikh Mohammed at the end of the previous season. Cecil was relying on Bosra Sham, a champion filly ridden by

Pat Eddery, to give him victory in this race, and in doing so would land him the trainers' championship, beating nearest competitor Saeed bin Suroor.

Early on in the race Frankie had to overcome the obstacle of stable companion Charnwood Forest ridden by Michael Kinane. Fortunately for Frankie, Michael let him past, leaving him to concentrate on Bosra Sham. Mark of Esteem accelerated in the final few furlongs leaving Bosra Sham for dead and giving Pat Eddery the shock of his life in the process. Already, Frankie had achieved a remarkable feat. He had won a Group 3, a Group 2 and a Group 1 race on one afternoon, against highly competitive fields. Even at this stage, Frankie had hit one of his excitably high moods, and felt as though all his birthdays had come at once.

The pressure was off, and Frankie was determined to enjoy the moment, running around the weighing room in a state of child-like euphoria before leaping from one interview to the next. Celebrations were only curtailed by the necessary interruption of the fourth race, the Tote Festival Handicap where he was to ride the Warning gelding Decorated Hero, priced at 7-1. This was also to be his only non-Godolphin ride of the day. Frankie wasn't feeling at all good about this race. The horse was known in John Gosden's yard as Square Wheels because he was such a bad mover. Weighing 9 st 13 lb certainly didn't help Frankie's cause; neither did being drawn in stall 22, right in the middle of the course.

Frankie soon realised the leaders had set off far too quickly and decided to stay so far back that he was last, thus allowing him to steadily ease Decorated Hero all the way over to the stands' rails and creep into contention. Frankie capitalised on his rivals' rushed start and claimed his fourth victory, three and a half lengths clear of his nearest rival!

At this stage of the day, Darren Yates had just lost his football match 4-0, and had made his way to the pub to discover what Frankie had achieved. Surely not even he could have anticipated Frankie winning the remaining three races.

A return to the royal blue colours of Godolphin for the fifth race saw Frankie mount Fatefully, in what was a competitive field of 18 runners. Although Fatefully stood a realistic chance, 7-4 seemed incredibly harsh odds considering the quality of the field. But the odds were so curtailed simply due to the sheer weight of money rolling forward on Frankie's mounts.

The Rosemary Stakes were to throw many complex challenges Frankie's way and test his skills to the limit. Shortly after the halfway point Frankie found himself blocked behind a wall of horses bunched near the stands rails. Eventually, Frankie decided to take a risk and charge Fatefully forward, pushing Pat Eddery on Questonia to check, thus effectively ending his race. With what seemed like a comfortable lead heading towards the final furlong, Frankie was tested to the limit by Abeyr ridden by his friend Ray Cochrane, who went on an ambitious late charge. Fatefully hung on by a whisker.

No sooner had Frankie begun to celebrate his fifth win of the day when a stewards' inquiry was announced, prompted by the uneasy overtaking of Pat Eddery's horse. Fortunately for Frankie, the stewards concluded that the interference was accidental, which was helped in part by Eddery's admission that his filly was beaten by the time the two touched.

Five races, five wins. One more victory and Frankie would equal Gordon Richards' record of winning six in a row. Unfortunately for Gordon, his remarkable achievement at Chepstow took place on a six-race card, but he could take some consolation in the fact he rode 12 consecutive winners over three days.

The sixth race, the Blue Seal Stakes, saw Frankie mount Lochsong's sister, Lochangel. His only real threat in the race was Pat Eddery riding Corsini, both suitably priced at 5-4. Trainer Ian Balding instructed Frankie to stay back behind the leaders and save something for the latter stages. Frankie had other ideas.

Lochangel leapt out of the stalls and it was clear to Frankie that over six furlongs it was better to let the horse follow her natural instincts and sprint. To do anything else would have been regarded as throwing away an early advantage. The threat from Corsini never really materialised, and when Pat Eddery's horse did come close in the final furlong, it was too little, too late. Race number six was well and truly in the bag, and Gordon Richards' record had been equalled.

The scene at the end of that race was one of sheer pandemonium. The Queen's representative at Ascot, Sir Michael Oswald, emerged with some champagne, and Frankie was thrown around in all directions by people wanting interviews.

A £1 accumulator would have been worth £8,365.50 at this stage, and that money would now fall on Fujiyama Crest, crassly priced at 2-1 for the final race of the day, the Gordon Carter Handicap. The horse had actually won the race with Frankie the previous year, but had just had a horrendous season and was not considered a serious contender for the race this time around, and the morning price was 12-1.

For the off-course market, it was essential to crush the odds against Fujiyama Crest so they laid heavily in the betting ring to bring down its starting price in a fabled desire to protect themselves. In this way, the mechanics of a tried and trusted system, which had served the nation's bookies so well for decades, broke down. Bookmakers in the ring realised they could lay 2-1 against a horse whose chances in reality were closer to 12-1. Instead of just cutting the odds lower still, they laid Fujiyama Crest for every penny they had, up to and including the value of their cars and houses.

This, in turn, immeasurably raised the stakes of the horse. Barry Dennis laid the horse to lose £23,000. During 30 years in the business, his previous biggest daily loss had been £5,000. This was to prove by far the worst day of his bookmaking career.

For Gary Wiltshire, who took a dauntless stand against a flood of money from betting shop chains, this would lead him to the brink of ruin.

The scene was set for the seventh and final race of the day. A once-in-a-lifetime drama at so many different levels was unfolding. From Frankie's point of view, it is difficult to make comparisons with any other sports of the magnitude of this achievement, if he won. Tiger Woods managing to birdie all 18 holes during a round comes close, and should he ever manage this, it should be held in equal esteem. Michael Schumacher winning every race on the calendar in one season is also in with a shout, but even so, he would be in a top-quality car for every one of those races, whereas Frankie was riding horses of vastly varying levels of ability for each of those seven races. Maybe Ian Botham turning around the Headingley test match of 1981 comes close. A remarkable achievement though that was, he was in no small part helped along by Bob Willis' superb bowling, something often overlooked by nostalgia lovers. No, there exist no obvious comparisons with what Frankie would achieve with a win on Fujiyama Crest.

Then there are the livelihoods at stake. These included the on-course bookies such as Gary Wiltshire and Barry Dennis, as well the big high-street bookmakers.

Add to this the romantic, life changing stories of John and Mary Bolton or Darren Yates nervously sipping his pint in anticipation of the final race. Across the country, at least £40 million was hanging on the result. The scene was set for something none of us is ever likely to live to see repeated.

Just before the race, Julian Wilson said goodbye to the hugely inflated television audience, and the BBC's coverage from Ascot came to an end. The British public were to be denied the chance to find out if the impossible really could be achieved. Frankie Dettori was to be denied the same courtesy given to Tim Henman when he plays a second-round match at

Wimbledon against a complete unknown that runs over into prime time hours.

Frankie walked towards the paddock to a standing ovation and raucous cheering. John Bolton took up his position on the grandstand steps near the finishing position, whilst his wife Mary continued to shop completely oblivious to what was going on.

Fujiyama Crest was given the worst stall of them all – stall one, on the stands' side, packed tightly against the rail. The race began steadily and Frankie gave the horse time to find his stride, and, without much effort, he edged across towards the far rail and claimed a narrow lead.

They eased downhill towards Swinley Bottom, extending their lead in the process. They turned right-handed and climbed back up the final mile. Frankie was struck by an overwhelming eruption of noise coming from the grandstand as they headed towards the finish, noise on a magnitude not normally heard at racecourses, and impossible for a jockey to blank out. However, Frankie's skills were to be put to the test one final time.

With just a few furlongs to go, Northern Fleet, ridden by Pat Eddery, began a late, and very threatening charge. With just one furlong to go, Fujiyama Crest was exhausted, barely managing to put one leg in front of the other. His tank was utterly empty, and he was almost unconscious. Eddery ensured the gap was narrowing all the time, and he made sure that Frankie and Fuji were going to be made to work for this victory.

Then, somehow, Fujiyama Crest conjured up a tiny

bit more energy to see them over the winning post. The impossible had happened. The crowd were, by now, ecstatic. They had witnessed something that had never happened before, and something most would dare not contemplate ever happening again. Frankie let out a huge scream, before going into a recluse-like state, struggling to come to terms with the magnitude of what he had achieved. This was to last several minutes before he returned to the winner's enclosure, did the customary flying dismount, and went into a hyperactive, trance-like state.

Fuji's racing manager John Ferguson was exhilarated, as Frankie flung his arms around him. Like everyone else at Ascot, he could not believe what had just happened, especially since Fuji had been so sluggish over the past year. Frankie then tore off his goggles and tossed them into the crowd, and then he soaked onlookers, who were on cloud nine and stunned by what they had witnessed, with champagne.

Frankie didn't have time to come down to earth during the next hour, the adrenaline still running high as he was pulled in all directions for interviews. Then came the all-important phone calls. Catherine had watched the first three races before going out, so Frankie got to break the news to her personally. His father took more convincing. He was in Tenerife and had been following the afternoon's racing on teletext. He assumed there had been a mistake and took some convincing from his son that this wasn't one of his wind-ups.

Frankie was generous with his time as he left Ascot,

signing thousands of autographs for the patient crowds, and listening to their stories of how they had made a profit that day by putting their faith in him.

Eventually, Frankie made his way back to the car where his driver had been waiting for him for some time. At last, Frankie had some time to himself, a chance to come back down to earth and come to terms with what had happened. Frankie made his driver wait ten minutes before driving off. To juxtapose the hysteria and elation of the previous hour, a dark cloud was approaching Frankie's mind, or, to put it more crudely, this was the onset of one of his bad moods.

There is no obvious reason why this should have been the case, other than the emotion of the occasion was just too much to handle. Frankie became irritated on the journey home by the sound of his mobile phone constantly ringing.

Soon after arriving home, his close friend from Godolphin Simon Crisford and his business manager Pete Burrell temporarily managed to lift his mood by cracking open the champagne and sitting down to watch a video of the day's events.

This was to be a brief interlude as soon after, Catherine announced that they had to go to a party that evening hosted by one of her old boyfriends. Frankie had endured a long, and, in many respects, difficult day and all he really wanted to do was to eat a meal and retire to bed, knowing full well he would be back racing at Ascot the following day. In the end, Frankie reached a compromise with Catherine. They would go to the party, but would not stay long.

Frankie was short and irascible with his wife on the journey home, and what should have been one of the happiest days of his life ended with husband and wife not speaking to each other.

This is a pertinent example of the extremes of Frankie's turbulent personality. The highs are very high, and the lows are very low. There are no in-betweens, and the mood can switch very quickly, without there being any obvious cause or trigger.

The impact this day had on Frankie's life is immeasurable, but it had just as an enormous an impact on the lives of several other people for whom life would never be the same again. Fate had been incredibly cruel for Gary Wiltshire that day. His heavy betting against the seven wins was not illogical, and he swears to this day he would do the same again. The cruel irony for him was that he was not even supposed to be at Ascot that day. He was actually on his way to Worcester when he hit heavy traffic on the M40, and phoned his clerk to tell him to turn around and head for Ascot instead.

With two races to go, he was still in profit. With one race left, he had only made a slight loss, not an especially bad day's work. Even then he was optimistic and very confident of turning the day around. He could lay 2-1 on a 16-1 shot, which sounds like a free holiday to any bookie. After all, there was no way Frankie was going to win all seven races, was there?

On the last race he took anything he could get, punters were queuing to get to his stand. He would have gone on forever had the whistle not blown to start the race. He knew he was in real trouble as they came into the straight. The unthinkable had happened, and he owed over £1 million to punters. It was going to be a long way back.

He sold his house, his cars, and everything of value he owned. He even resorted to selling Christmas paper in Oxford Street to make ends meet. That same night, he went to work at Milton Keynes dogs, his first bet being for just £1, and so the long, painful journey back to financial stability begun. The following day, he returned to Ascot, where not one punter would place a bet with him, thinking it would be impossible for him to honour his debts.

To his credit, he settled every bet, and vowed he would do the same again. They say that every cloud has a silver lining, and this can certainly be said of Gary Wiltshire. It could even be argued, ten years after the event, that this day was to be the making, rather than the breaking of him, and looking at the direction his life has taken in the intervening years, the fame he gained on that day appears to have opened doors of opportunity for him that would otherwise have remained firmly shut.

As time went on, he became increasingly disillusioned by the growing dominance of the online betting exchanges. He had also come to the conclusion that racing's big personalities were fading fast, and with overall attendances at the country's 59 racecourses falling, he felt a change in direction was needed.

A chance meeting with Joe Scanlon, the managing director of Totesport, turned Gary's life around. The Tote was going through a period of massive change, going from a dated, state-owned betting pool to an entrepreneurial, multi-faceted bookmaking chain to rival the big three. Yes, for the first time in his life Gary would be working for somebody other than himself, but there seems little doubt this was to prove the right decision.

He made his debut for the Tote at Royal Ascot in 2005, alongside blonde Tote girl Pam Sharman, who was to become his regular raceday companion. Whilst they might look like the ultimate beauty-and-the-beast team to an outsider, in truth Pam was the brains behind the operation, and had been in charge of Tote credit, looking after the highest concentration of UK credit customers in British racing. The Tote is going through the biggest transformation in its history and is making a serious impact on the industry, and Gary Wiltshire is at the forefront of that change.

For this likeable, witty, larger-than-life character, who suffered so terribly on the back of Frankie's success, life has turned out just fine. This is surely a shining example of the karma principle of 'what goes around, comes around' in action, and Gary's integrity of paying out to every winning bet has, in turn, paid huge dividends for him in the long term.

For Britain's most well-known and loudest on-course bookmaker, Barry Dennis, the consequences were not nearly as catastrophic but were still extremely painful. As Fujiyama Crest crossed the winning line, he was standing on his stool, in a trance, oblivious to the surrounding uproar.

He drove home in silence, his staff too frightened to

speak. Upon arriving home, he was greeted by his wife's customary cheery welcome. 'Good day?' she enquired. He told his wife that Frankie had won all seven winners. 'Fantastic!' she said. 'What a great achievement.' She was clearly unacquainted with the impact such an accomplishment would have upon her husband's living. Barry fell into the chair, sobbing. Whilst his wealth had taken a significant dent, it wouldn't be long before 'The Bismarck' returned to his usual, over-the-top self, for which he is renowned.

This was a very rare bad day for the bookmakers, and one where life-changing sums of money were won by ordinary punters. For Darren Yates, the hard times were over. His shrewd investment had landed him a cheque for £550,000. On the following Monday morning, instead of getting up to face another hard, poorly-paid week as a joiner, he found himself sitting on the GMTV sofa being presented with his winning cheque by Frankie himself.

Darren has invested his money wisely in the intervening years, and has showed little of the perceived recklessness that saw him constantly backing Dettori when he couldn't really afford to. Today, he has doubled the size of his business and moved into a comfortable house. He has even dabbled in owning horses. Fittingly he called his first horse Seventh Heaven. This one failed to make the grade, though he has since enjoyed success with Royal Dome and Natsmagirl.

For John and Mary Bolton, their win was the anniversary present from heaven. John had managed to miscalculate his winnings, and thought he had won £300,000. In fact, he had done far better than that. In theory, they should have won £900,000 but Ladbrokes had inoculated themselves against these freak occurrences with a maximum payout policy of £500,000 – still a far higher amount than John thought he'd won.

There were dozens more instances of punters winning over £100,000 on that day, and even those who had staked as little as 50p on accumulators found they had won thousands of pounds.

A bad day for the bookies all round? Well, almost – there was one notable exception. Bookie Peter Saxton placed a stake of £32.70 at Corals and found himself winning £247,000. Talk about hedging his bets!

For the record, anyone putting together the seven winners in an accumulator would have received combined odds of 25,095-1!

After a few days in the limelight the lucky winners returned to their ordinary lifestyles, albeit more comfortable ones than before. But for Frankie, and the racing industry as a whole, nothing would ever be the same again.

His fame was to immediately extend from that of an immensely popular jockey, well-liked by punters and the racing fraternity as a whole, to a national media phenomenon, appealing to sections of the public who would not normally take any interest at all in racing. This massive achievement, combined with a naturally flamboyant personality, would open windows of opportunity and see him become a marketing brand in

Always keen to seize the day, here he poses with the £110,000 scarlet two-seat Ferrari Modena that he bought to cheer himself up during his recuperation.

Above: Frankie showing his delight at being awarded an MBE in the New Year's Honours list in 2001.

Below left: With Foreign Secretary Robin Cook after being presented his MBE.

Below right: Ray Cochrane holding The Queen's Commendation for Bravery, Newmarket January 2002. He was awarded this honour by the Queen for his extraordinary acts of bravery during the plane crash.

Frankie standing in front of the life-size bronze statue celebrating the five-year anniversary of his Magnificent Seven win, Ascot 2001.

Above: Frankie with fellow jockeys at the moving opening ceremony of the Breeders' Cup October 2001.

Below: Winning the Breeders' Cup 2001 on Fantastic Light.

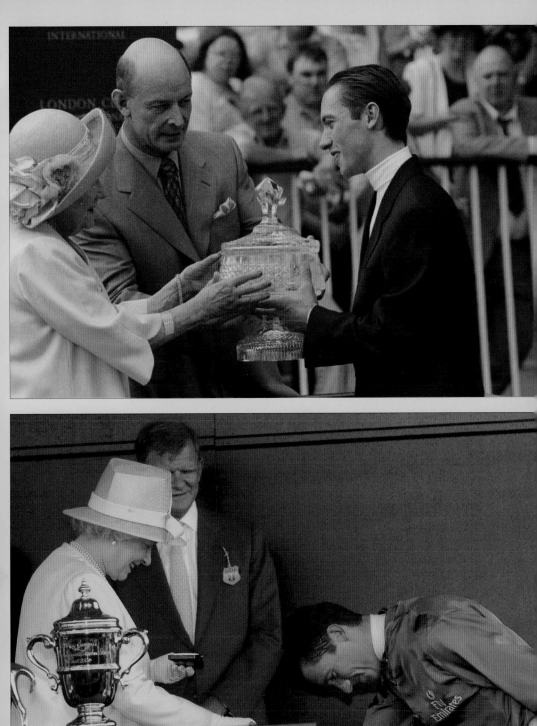

Above: Collecting a trophy from the Queen Mother at Ascot, 1998.

Below: The Queen presented Frankie with his trophy after he won the King George VI and Queen Elizabeth Diamond Stakes on Doyen at Ascot, 24 July 2004.

As a unique sports personality Frankie became a firm favourite on our television screens. As well as captaining a team on *A Question of Sport*, he guest-starred on the panel of sports quiz *They Think It's All Over* with Jonathan Ross and Boris Becker (*above*) and showed his funny side by horsing around on *The Paul O'Grady show* (*below*).

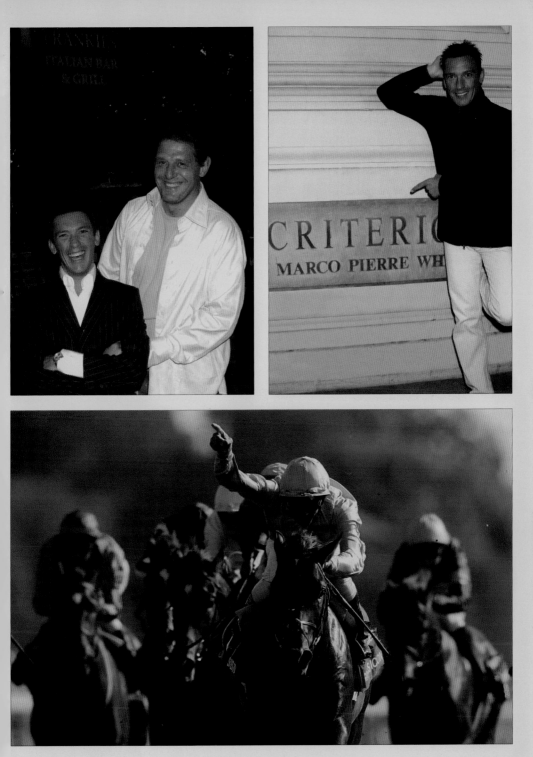

Above left: Frankie with chef and close friend Marco Pierre White at the opening of their new restaurant in Chiswick High Street, September 2005.

Above right: Outside the Criterion, the venue for his latest restaurant venture in 2006.

Below: Winning the Ladbrokes St Leger Stakes race on Sixties Icon at York in September 2006 gave him a phenomenal hundredth win of the season.

Frankie showed his support of his home country by painting the colours of the national flag on his cheek to celebrate their 2006 World Cup Win.

his own right, to rival that of David Beckham and Tiger Woods. Nothing even remotely comparable has happened to any jockey before or since, and the impact was immediate and continues to this day.

Frankie awoke on the Sunday morning to find a *Daily Mail* reporter in his house, who had somehow managed to walk straight in during the night. After this, he knew that things would never be the same again.

He went for a stroll to pick up the papers to find he was dominating both the front and back pages – something no jockey, even multiple Grand National winners had managed before. That morning, he attended Mass at Newmarket's Catholic Church, then headed to Ascot once again for what was to be a far quieter day for riding winners, managing just the one win on Altamura.

His mobile phone didn't stop ringing all day, with requests for interviews, product endorsements and other promotional activities. An urgent meeting with manager Pete Burrell was needed. Between them they decided it was in Frankie's interests, and the interests of the racing industry as a whole, to milk it for all it was worth. This opportunity would never come around again. Provided it didn't clash with the racing schedule, Frankie was up for almost anything.

Within days Frankie found himself in Downing Street for a reception for sports stars, hosted by the-then Prime Minister John Major. Frankie was in awe of the company in which he was mixing, which included Olympic rowers and multiple gold-medal-winners Sir

Steve Redgrave and Matthew Pinsent, champion boxers 'Prince' Naseem Hamed and Frank Bruno, and most of England's football team.

When he met the Prime Minister, he found out that Mr Major had watched six of the seven races on television and had been mesmerised by the afternoon's events. Thankfully for Frankie the reception didn't last long. Despite his new-found celebrity, the next day's riding had to be his priority and he was all too aware of the need to get a good night's sleep and to shed a few pounds in the morning.

Combining riding and being a celebrity has always been a fine balancing act for Frankie. At the height of the season it is a seven-day-a-week job, so daytime chat shows and requests to open shops are usually turned down. Being a celebrity is a job for the evenings, after the races are over.

He appeared on *Parkinson* one evening and told him he'd be taking over his job when he retired from riding. Would the guests be able to get a word in edgeways? More was to follow. Not long after he was asked to present *Top of the Pops*. Luckily the recording schedule coincided with a rare day off riding for Frankie, so he could accept it. It turned out to be tough going. He spent a whole day rehearsing his links, but in the end he proved a good sport and his efforts went down well.

But Frankie's command of the English language was to cause him occasional embarrassment. He was certainly fluent by this time, but he has, from time to time, spoken without really thinking through what he was saying. One notorious example occurred during his interview with Sybil Ruscoe on BBC Radio Five Live, shortly after he rode the Magnificent Seven. Sybil asked Frankie why it was necessary for jockeys to carry whips. Frankie's explanation was that a jockey without a whip was like a carpenter without a spanner!

Then came the commercial endorsements, again, completely unprecedented for anyone involved in the racing industry. The most conventional contract came from the Tote, who offered Frankie £50,000 to promote the brand, later renewed at £60,000. The rest had nothing whatsoever to do with the racing industry, and illustrate the extent to which Frankie had become a commercial brand, exposing himself, and racing as a whole, to a whole new audience in the process.

Frankie found himself working on advertising campaigns for One-2-One, T-mobile, McDonalds and Royal Doulton. But his favourite commercial venture was his association with Alfa Romeo. For a relatively small amount of endorsement work, he would receive three cars, twice a year – one for his wife, one for his petrol-headed agent, and the third for himself.

Following all the publicity, Frankie has also become a successful businessman in his own right. Surely none of this would have been possible had it not been for the remarkable events of Saturday, 28 September 1996.

CHAPTER 11

The Best Job in Racing

The remainder of the 1996 season brought mixed fortunes for Frankie. Any hopes of being champion jockey had vanished long ago, due to his lengthy absence through injury during the summer, but there were some worthwhile victories worth noting before the season came to an end.

There were two more Group 1 victories, the first coming when Frankie rode Bahamian Bounty, trained by David Loder in the Middle Park Stakes at Newmarket, followed by victory in the Prix Marcel Boussac at Longchamp on the John Gosden-trained Ryafan.

After a disappointing Arc, Frankie headed to Milan to take part in the Gran Premio de Jockey Club, where he clocked up yet another victory on Shantou. The Breeders' Cup, which was held for the first and thus far only time outside America, at Woodbine in Toronto, Canada, saw Frankie ride Mark Of Esteem in his farewell performance, but the horse failed to get going and he failed to end a glittering and highly rewarding career in fitting style.

Frankie was approached by Michael Stoute to ride Singspiel for the first time in the Japan Cup. Having analysed his performances in such races as the Breeders' Cup Classic where he finished a close second, Michael was convinced the horse could only just cope with twelve furlongs. His instructions to Frankie were to count to ten when he felt the need to accelerate before making his move. When the time came, Frankie managed to count to two before losing patience and going for it. He held on by a nose and collected an enormous £1,093,662. Frankie collected a new car in addition to his cut, which he sold at a discount because he couldn't take it out of the country. Not a bad day's work nonetheless.

Frankie managed one more Group 1 win before the year ended, this time on Luso, trained by Clive Brittain, in the Hong Kong Vase at Sha Tin Racecourse.

However, a few days later at the same course Frankie endured yet another injury that could have put paid to his career, or even his life, when he rode Magic Power. Shortly into the race, another runner clipped his heels, sending jockey Jackie Tse tumbling to the ground, and Magic Power onto the running rails. Frankie went flying from the horse. Magic Power somersaulted past Frankie, fracturing his foreleg in the process, and had to be put down.

Frankie was stretchered off the course and taken to hospital. He was severely shaken but had only suffered a damaged wrist and severe bruising. Fortunately, he was well enough to fly home to London as planned.

After Christmas Frankie headed for Al Quoz once more where he spent the rest of the winter in the balmy heat of Dubai riding out for Godolphin. When the Dubai World Cup came round once more, Frankie rode Tamayaz to victory for Godolphin, getting his season off to the best possible start and making Godolphin's presence felt at the event the Sheikh had done so much to initiate. Frankie rode a total of seven winners in Dubai before heading back to Newmarket in time for the start of the flat season in April.

However, it wouldn't be too long before Frankie discovered that Godolphin having a retainer on him did occasionally have its drawbacks. Frankie and John Gosden had been preparing Benny The Dip for a ride in the Derby. The horse was in excellent shape and both Frankie and John knew he stood a very real chance of success in the race. This was made all the more clear when Frankie rode him into second place in the Thresher Classic Trial at Sandown in April.

Naturally John would have wanted Frankie to ride the horse on the big day, and thought he was in with a chance of getting him since Godolphin didn't have a serious contender lined up. However, eleven days before the Derby, Bold Demand won a maiden for Godolphin at Sandown and the Sheikh decided the horse was ready for the Derby, and insisted Frankie be the jockey.

The Sheikh is unashamedly bold about horses' progress and is not afraid to chance them in big races. He has been proved right many times and his decision this time was by no means reckless. But there is no denying it was a lost opportunity for Frankie, who missed one of his best ever chances to ride a Derby winner.

Willie Ryan replaced Frankie and rode Benny The Dip to a spectacular victory, holding off a late challenge from Silver Patriarch. Frankie was left way back in ninth place. The meeting at Epsom was not entirely fruitless, though, as Frankie managed to win the valuable consolation prize by sealing victory in the Coronation Cup on Singspiel.

He was naturally delighted to be back riding at Royal Ascot after the frustration of having to watch the previous year's meeting from his living room with his arm in plaster. He managed two notable victories, winning the Queen Anne Stakes on Allied Forces for Godolphin and in the Group 1 St James' Palace Stakes on Sheikh Mohammed's Starborough, trained by David Loder.

Later that month he found himself taking the St Leger on Shantou, followed by a victory in Italy at the Gran Premio Di Milano. The same meeting saw him score his only victory thus far in the Italian Oaks on the French horse Nicole Pharly.

And, in what was a memorable June, he rode Luso in the Deutschland-Preis at Düsseldorf. Luso had brought him victory in Hong Kong at the tail end of the previous season and Frankie knew he had a decent chance of winning on the Newmarket trainer Clive

Brittain's horse. Frankie won the race emphatically and Luso became only the second ever British-trained horse to win this race, the first being Ibn Bey in 1990, trained by Paul Cole and ridden by Frankie's arch-rival, Richard Quinn.

Frankie was back on board Singspiel in the Juddmonte International at York, a race he'd won twelve months earlier on Halling, which would pit the Coronation Cup winner against two Derby winners in the shape of Desert King and Benny The Dip. Frankie and Singspiel stormed home to victory and this confirmed Singspiel's status as the greatest horse in the country, and amongst the best in the world.

Sadly, this would turn out to be Singspiel's swansong, as later that year he was flown to America and sustained a serious leg injury running round Hollywood Park course in preparation for a shot at the Breeders' Cup. Fortunately he was saved for stud, but Frankie was greatly saddened to see what he considered to be one of the all-time greats retired before he had the chance to prove his credentials against the best horses in the world.

Frankie rounded off the 1997 season in Britain in late September by winning the Fillies' Mile at Ascot on the Luca Cumani-trained Gloriosa. This was Frankie's second victory for Luca in this race, having won on Shamsir back in 1990.

Frankie rode a total of 176 winners in Britain that season, but the year was to come to something of a controversial end. Under the totting up procedure, a lengthy ban was coming and Frankie was well aware of it. Once he'd reached a tally of fifteen days' ban during a season, a lengthy ban of twenty-one days would follow. He knew the rules, and knew that it would be better to get his ban out of the way now, at the end of the season, than have it hanging over him for the start of the following year. In other words, if he was to be banned now all he would miss would be some minor all-weather races in November and the Japan Cup, whereas if he was to reach the tally of fifteen days early in the next season he'd be banned for some important early season races.

In order to take control of the situation for himself, on 31 October at Newmarket, Frankie began a race with the specific intention of being banned as a result. During the final stages of the race he pulled the whip through to his left hand and made his mount Baajil drift sharply across the horses on his inside. Frankie could hear Michael Hills, his brother Richard and John Reid all shouting in disbelief, but Frankie had achieved his objective.

In the weighing room after the race, he took a tirade of abuse from the other jockeys. Frankie's behaviour was completely out of character. They couldn't believe what they were hearing when Frankie told them the truth – that he'd done it on purpose. He made it clear he didn't want any of them speaking up for him in the inquiry.

Sure enough, Frankie was referred to Portman Square and collected a three-week ban. His cunning plan had worked, and the slate was wiped clean for the start of the 1998 season. Frankie had turned the Jockey Club's rules to his advantage.

During that winter in Al Quoz, one horse from the Godolphin stable really stood out. Cape Verdi was in superb shape and a hard-working horse who responded well to the jockeys who rode out on her. She was eager and hungry for success. Her trainer, Saeed bin Suroor and Frankie both agreed she was in pristine shape for the upcoming 1,000 Guineas a few days later.

On the day of the race, she eased down to the start in a relaxed and calm fashion, kept perfectly still in the stalls, and moved through the race in textbook style, coming home unchallenged five lengths clear of Shahtoush. The Sheikh had seen enough to enter Cape Verdi for the Derby, but the more conservative-minded Frankie would have preferred to enter her for the Oaks, where she was a cert to win.

A decent substitute for the Oaks was found in the shape of Bahr. On the day, Frankie rode well and held back until the final furlong before launching his onslaught on leader Midnight Line. He had left it slightly too late, however, and was overtaken by Mick Kinane on Shahtoush. Things may well have been different if Frankie had accelerated a furlong further back. However, Frankie did eventually enjoy success on Bahr, winning that year's Ribblesdale Stakes at Royal Ascot.

1998 looked like being the year Frankie was going to win the Derby. He couldn't have asked for a horse in better shape than Cape Verdi. Everything was looking good, and everyone involved with the Godolphin operation saw this as their first chance to secure victory in the Derby. However, it wasn't to be, as Frankie got locked into an unpleasant battle with his adversary, Richard Quinn, on Courteous. Richard's horse gave Cape Verdi a severe bashing as they went wide, and they kept clashing every few strides, which inevitably caused Cape Verdi pain in her ribs. The race was eventually won by High-Rise, trained by Luca and ridden by Frankie's friend Olivier Peslier.

The Royal Ascot of that summer was to be a vintage one for Frankie and Godolphin. It was Frankie's chance to secure the Gold Cup on Kayf Tara. Frankie knew that the race was likely to be a battle between Kayf Tara and Double Trigger with Darryll Holland riding. He had learnt his lesson from the Oaks and there was no danger of him leaving it too late to challenge this time. Frankie let his rival do all the hard work, seeing off the other horses one by one, before beginning his assault and stealing victory by a neck.

The Godolphin stable was on a roll, which continued when the stable took a clean sweep at the Coral-Eclipse at Sandown. Frankie won the race on Daylami, with stable companions Faithful Son and Central Park taking second and third respectively.

Three weeks later at Ascot, Frankie was back on board Swain in the King George VI and Queen Elizabeth Diamond Stakes, undeterred by the horse's defeat at Royal Ascot the previous month which had left some questioning whether he still had what it takes. The race is an annual contest between Classic horses and the older generation, and with Swain being a veteran, nobody could be sure if he could still manage such a tough challenge. Frankie had made the mistake of declining Swain in favour of Singspiel for this race the previous year, but he certainly made up for it this time round, taking Swain into the lead with just over a furlong left, leaving the Derby winner High-Rise back in second place.

Swain had silenced his critics, but the old man wasn't finished yet, as Frankie rode him to victory in the Irish Champion Stakes six weeks later.

At the Juddmonte International at York, Frankie was involved in a thrilling race, which could easily have ended up as a three-way dead heat. To the naked eye, it certainly seemed as though three horses crossed the line together – Frankie on Faithful Son, Pat Eddery on One So Wonderful and Kieren Fallon on Chester House. In the end, Pat's horse prevailed by a short head.

However, all three jockeys involved in the riveting tussle had let their enthusiasm get the better of them and received suspensions for whip offences minutes later. This time, Frankie protested his innocence, claiming that he only ever uses the whip to encourage horses to do the job for which they are bred, not to beat them up.

By now, Godolphin was becoming an increasingly confident, well-oiled operation. In September, Frankie and Godolphin secured a Group 2 victory on French soil, winning the Prix de la Salamandre on Aljabr. This autumn, as every autumn, they began their pursuit of promising young horses that may be available to buy. A rumour was circulating that there was a young colt at

Newmarket with the sort of talent that only comes around on a few occasions in any one person's lifetime.

His name was Yazzer and he was trained by David Loder and owned by the Sheikh. David made little secret of his ambition for Yazzer and, after seeing him on the gallops at Newmarket, Frankie could understand his enthusiasm. Shortly before he made his debut, the Sheikh took the decision to rename the horse, giving him the grand title Dubai Millennium.

The horse was to make his debut at Yarmouth in late October. Under normal circumstances, Frankie would have been expected to ride the Godolphin horse Blue Snake in the race. But these were not normal circumstances, and the Sheikh gave him permission to switch to Dubai Millennium, who went on to win with incredible style, giving an aura of unbelievable confidence with it. The manner of this victory confirmed what Frankie and the Sheikh already knew – this horse was something very special.

In November, Frankie had one of the worst experiences of his career, and one that would take a long time for him to come to terms with. It came without warning, there was no way anyone was expecting this, and it could easily have led to the end of his career with Godolphin.

He set off for America to ride Swain in what was to be the horse's swansong, the Breeders' Cup. But he wasn't feeling at full strength, having picked up a nasty cough during a dusty run across an open ranch in Argentina on a short break on his way to the States. Frankie believed the key to success was not to allow

Swain to be drawn into a battle with Silver Charm, who had beaten Swain by the narrowest of margins in the Dubai World Cup in March.

The first half of the race went perfectly, with Frankie tucked nicely behind the leader, Cornado's Quest. As the race quickened, Gary Stevens began his assault on Silver Charm and gained the lead with a furlong left. Frankie took Swain wide, thinking this would be enough to snatch the lead. He hit Swain more frequently than he should have and Swain responded by charging sharply right-handed towards the stands. The one key mistake Frankie made was whipping Swain with his left hand as the horse was moving to the right, but this does not tell the whole story as to why Swain freaked out, blowing the race to finish a disappointing third.

It is entirely possible that Swain was startled by the floodlights and this caused him to react in this way, but many horses riding were not used to the floodlights and they didn't do anything like this. It was a freak incident, and the whole truth about what really caused Swain's behaviour has never been uncovered.

But despite the lack of evidence that Frankie was largely to blame, the knives were out. The whole world seemed to be against him, and he took a barrage of abuse from the press and the spectators. Frankie lost his rag, and told everyone he'd ridden a diabolical race, despite knowing that it might not have been entirely his fault. Sections of the press had been after Frankie for a long time, and they weren't going to let this opportunity to destroy his reputation go.

Frankie took a flight home as soon as possible. Once on the plane, he broke down in tears in Catherine's lap, believing his days riding for Godolphin were over. One bad race had undone years of hard work. He was convinced there was no way back.

The following day Frankie took a phone call from the Sheikh telling him not to worry about the stick he had taken in that day's newspapers, and that everyone at Godolphin backed him one hundred per cent. But the season was over now, and he had all winter to dwell on it.

When he arrived in Dubai at the start of February, one unnamed person at Godolphin was not so forgiving and made every effort to make Frankie's life as miserable as possible. Frankie took this abuse for two months. He may have made a serious mistake, although it probably wasn't entirely his fault. What is certain is that he didn't deserve to be made a scapegoat in this way after all the wins he'd ridden for the stable in the previous few seasons.

Only Catherine knew the extent of Frankie's torment at this time. During the day he would seem fine, but most evenings he would break down in tears, unable to cope with the abuse he was getting. Eventually, he cracked during a meal in a restaurant with a group of friends, sobbing uncontrollably. Nobody except Catherine knew what it was all about.

The following morning Catherine took him to see Simon Crisford to tell him how he was really feeling. A meeting was arranged with the Sheikh straight away. Frankie made his feelings clear to the Sheikh, telling him that his confidence was in pieces and that if he wasn't happy with his performances it was in all their interests to part company. Things just couldn't go on as they had during the past two months.

The Sheikh stopped Frankie in full flow, and put him straight about things. He told him he should never forget he was the jockey who rode all seven winners at Ascot, and that he should carry on – he had his full backing.

In truth, it was never the Sheikh that was the cause of Frankie's misery, but he felt hugely reassured that he was not going to fire him on the grounds of one bad performance. It was time to move on, and this experience made Frankie a stronger person.

CHAPTER 12

The Best Horse in the World

1999 was to be one of the most successful, yet one of the most controversial years of Frankie's career. It began in disastrous style when he finished last on Derby-winning High-Rise in the Dubai World Cup.

But things improved when the British flat season got underway and he rode a surprise winner in Island Sands in the 2,000 Guineas for Godolphin. In late May came victory in the Italian Derby, again for Godolphin, this time on Mukhalif.

Six days later it was time to test Dubai Millennium in the Derby. This was surely to be Frankie's best ever chance of winning the race, and it was an opportunity not to be missed. In truth, Dubai Millennium was probably too quick for the Derby and he was rushed to get there. By the time they were on the straight he was struggling to hold his position. The race was won by

Kieren Fallon on Oath, trained by Henry Cecil, who had by now entered into a bitter rivalry with the Sheikh over the sale of a number of horses.

Frankie's season soon got back on track when he rode Daylami to a Group 1 double, first at the Coronation Cup at Epsom, followed by victory in the King George at Ascot, which saw him ease home by five lengths to another Godolphin horse, Nedawi.

The following few months saw Frankie and Godolphin score a number of victories in key races including Aljabr in the Sussex Stakes, Diktat in the Haydock Sprint Cup and Prix Maurice de Gheest and Kayf Tara in the Irish St Leger. In July, Frankie rode Dubai Millennium to another important victory in the Maisons-Laffitte over the less enduring distance of ten furlongs.

August saw Frankie testing Dubai Millennium on French soil, securing the Prix Jacques le Marois at Deauville in a competitive field. Soon it was time to test Dubai Millennium in the Queen Elizabeth II Stakes at Ascot.

The biggest problem was always going to be controlling the horse. In the early stages, Frankie didn't want to take on the leader, Gold Academy, but Dubai Millennium pulled fiercely and holding him back proved a massive challenge for Frankie. After the halfway point, Frankie felt exhausted and decided to let him go. Dubai Millennium charged ahead leaving everything behind her for dead, winning by a massive six lengths without even being pushed at all by Frankie. The Sheikh celebrated the victory by declaring

Dubai Millennium to be the best horse Godolphin had ever had, and on that performance it was hard to argue.

The Irish Champion Stakes clashed with the St Leger, but Godolphin's priority was Frankie's outing at Leopardstown on Daylami. On paper the race looked like being a clash between Daylami and Royal Anthem ridden by Gary Stevens, who had put in an impressive win at York the previous month. Royal Anthem took the lead early on but was unable to pull away from the pack. On the home straight Frankie spotted a gap next to the rails and charged past. He called out to Gary to ask him how much he had left. When there was no response, he knew he'd got him. Daylami won the race by a massive nine lengths, leaving Dazzling Park in second. Unfortunately Daylami failed to repeat this performance in the Arc when he began to gurgle five furlongs out, but this wasn't the end of her season.

In September Frankie was involved in the most unpleasant episode of his career, when he admitted he had taken diuretic drugs to keep his weight down before the Jockey Club banned such substances the previous June.

The controversy began when an amateur rider, Paul Fitzsimons, claimed that many apprentices were ignoring the Jockey Club ban. Kieren Fallon added fuel to the fire by declaring, 'Bulimia is the only way left for jockeys now that Dr Michael Turner [chief medical adviser to the Jockey Club] has taken most of the medication off the shelf.'

The story became a lengthy feature on the BBC's *Newsnight* programme, where Frankie gave an interview as part of a report on the subject. When asked if he had ever taken the banned substances, he said, 'I took Lasix, pee pills, diuretics, laxatives; all sorts.' When asked whether he still took pills, he said, 'I try not to.'

Peter Burrell responded by saying that he was considering taking legal action against the BBC over the contents of the press release used to publicise the programme, though nothing came of it. The Jockey Club, for its part, tried to put the record straight on the impact the ban had had for the sport. Spokesman John Maxse said, 'Since the ban there have been no positives. Those who tested positive for diuretics before the ban came in were all young riders and none was a top jockey. To infer that drug taking and the use of diuretics in racing is rife is totally misleading.'

There was a furore lasting a few days, though in reality the story was a storm in a teacup. There is no suggestion Frankie has ever done anything improper to keep his weight down and before the ban came in his methods were no worse than those of other jockeys.

Frankie's attention soon turned to the Breeders' Cup Turf race at Gulfstream Park in Florida in November. But first he headed to Australia to take part in the Melbourne Cup. Upon landing, he discovered that his ride, Kayf Tara, had been pulled out of the race following a setback, so he was left to run Central Park instead. The horse was dismissed as something of a no-hoper, but managed to give a brave fight before tiring out twenty yards from home. Even Frankie was impressed with how well he had run that day.

His mind, though was focussed on returning to America for the first time since the Swain incident, and he was eager to end the European 34-year drought in the big race. Frankie took a great deal of stick from the American press in the build up to the race, with snide remarks such as to watch out for the lights.

Frankie had one advantage over his critics. He knew how good Daylami had been that season and, provided there was no repeat of the Arc, he knew he was in with a very good chance of securing victory.

When the race began, his priority was to get an early position close to the rail, which would be pivotal to his success. Once he'd managed that he dropped in just behind the leaders. Royal Anthem eased past them but Frankie wasn't unduly concerned by this, gradually upping the pace on Daylami and waiting patiently for a gap to appear. When it came he gave the horse a few snacks and he charged clear at lightning pace. Nobody stood a chance against the dynamic duo of Frankie and Daylami, rounding up what had been a vintage year.

In the press conference that followed, Frankie couldn't wait to rub their noses in it after the stick he'd taken the previous year. He asked them if they wanted to talk about Swain now, but there was no answer to that. Frankie had well and truly silenced his critics in spectacular style. This was a night, and a year to remember.

This was also the season when Frankie had to face up to the reality that Mattie was no longer well enough to cope with the demands of the job of being Frankie's agent. It was Frankie who had paid for him to have a heart bypass two years earlier, but he was in frail health and the demands of the job were higher than ever, so Frankie suggested he step down.

Despite Mattie's enforced retirement, Frankie realised he still owed him a debt of gratitude for all he had done for him, especially during his early years, and they have stayed close friends. Mattie was replaced by Andrew Stringer, who only stayed in the job until Ray Cochrane's enforced retirement from riding the following year, which resulted in him becoming Frankie's agent.

Frankie was back in action in March when, as was now the norm, he'd spent the latter part of the winter riding out for Al Quoz. The plan was to enter Dubai Millennium in the upcoming Dubai World Cup. Everybody was in awe of his potential – this truly was something quite special.

The Sheikh decided that Dubai Millennium needed the chance to get used to the kick-back from the dirt surface, and so was entered into the Maktoum Challenge in early March. Frankie spent the first half of the race tucked behind horses to get him used to have him get used to having sand kicked in his face. Then Frankie let him go and he won four and a half lengths clear of Lear Spear. Despite Frankie holding him back, he set a new course record of 1 minute 59.6 seconds. The potential of this horse was truly frightening.

Frankie wasn't allowed near the Dubai Millennium until the final few days before the Dubai World Cup. There was no stopping the him, he covered five furlongs in 59 seconds, leaving everyone at Godolphin furious with Frankie, convinced the horse had run his race on the gallops. In the case of most horses, this would've been true, but this was no ordinary horse.

Frankie was so confident of his chances he'd persuaded Gianfranco and Christine to fly over for the race. His confidence increased further when he discovered he'd drawn an outside stall, which would result in far less kick-back.

After a solid start, they found themselves out in front after a furlong. This wasn't as Frankie had planned it, but they were into a rhythm and there was no point in holding back. Even though they were up against some of the best horses in the world, including several Americans, who are far more used to the dirt, the result never seemed in any doubt.

Dubai Millennium eased round the bend, head down, charging along, steadily increasing his lead all the time, requiring little encouragement from Frankie. When they were clearly out in front, Frankie asked for a little bit more, and Dubai Millennium charged at lightning pace, leaving the others out of sight, covering ten furlongs in 1 minute 59.5 seconds.

The Dubai crowed loved this horse – he was like one of their own. Frankie was confronted by a wall of noise as they fought their way to the winner's circle. This was like nothing he'd ever seen before. After an ultra-enthusiastic flying dismount, Frankie headed to the weighing room before returning and riding Dubai Millennium bareback in front of the grandstand.

The first prize in the race was a mind-boggling £2,195,122, of which £219,000 went straight into

Frankie's pocket. He also received a gold whip covered in diamonds. When he returned to Britain, he watched the video of the race again and again while running on the treadmill each morning. Frankie felt on top of the world, and couldn't believe his luck in having the fortune to be at the peak of his powers as a jockey when the once-in-a-lifetime horse, Dubai Millennium, was around.

CHAPTER 13

Taking the World by Storm

During his recovery from the horrific plane crash in June 2000, one thought dominated Frankie's mind – riding Dubai Millennium again. His target was to ride him in at Deauville in mid August. This would mean pushing himself to recover as quickly as possible, and inevitably rushing back more quickly than would have been ideal. But he needed a goal, an incentive to keep him going during the difficult and painful weeks of physiotherapy and recuperation that lay ahead.

His spirits lifted when, against the orders of the doctors and his wife, he travelled to Royal Ascot to see Dubai Millennium in the Prince of Wales's Stakes. Frankie's temporary replacement, Jerry Bailey, guided Dubai Millennium to a spectacular victory in what became a no-contest. Frankie was overcome with emotion as his favourite horse of all time crossed the winning line, and this increased his desire still further to be back in time for Deauville.

Frankie was still having to walk slowly and so trailed into the paddock way behind the rest of the Godolphin team. As he passed the main grandstand he received a rapturous round of applause from the crowd. It felt good to be there, and it brought home to Frankie the high level of affection felt for him by the British public.

These factors kept him going and thinking positive over the weeks that followed. It was going to be a tough time and would require Frankie pushing through the pain barrier in the rush back to fitness. In the first few weeks, the biggest problem was the huge blisters that appeared on his hands because of the constant use of crutches.

The day of his visit to Royal Ascot, Frankie achieved one other notable feat. He travelled there by helicopter, the first time he had taken to the skies since his accident. It was a brave decision, but was probably the correct one. The nature of his job meant he would have to take to fly again sooner or later and it was probably better to get the ordeal out of the way before he'd had too much time to dwell on it and cause his fear to increase further.

Shortly afterwards he got on a plane for the first time, as he went for a break with Gianfranco in Sardinia. Frankie coped remarkably well with both flights, although there was no hiding his relief when they landed safely. To this day, Frankie gets nervous if something doesn't go entirely smoothly during a flight. Landing in bad weather, turbulence and other things that are an inevitable part of frequent flying cause him a degree of distress, but considering what he has been through, and the speed at which he got back on board a helicopter, it can be said he has come to terms with his fears brought about by that terrible accident.

During his time in Sardinia, Frankie was unable to do much other than bathe in salt water and walk gently over the sand, and even this proved exceedingly painful, but a necessary challenge if he was to make it back in time for Deauville.

Whilst in Sardinia he received the surprise news that he'd been recommended for an MBE in the New Year's Honours. Danish goalkeeper Peter Schmeichel was to receive the award as well. The hardest part was always going to be keeping the news quiet all the way until January.

Once he'd returned home, it wasn't long before he was riding out once more, despite there still being a long way to go until he was fully recovered. He protected his heavily-swollen right ankle by putting all the pressure on his left leg. His ankle remained wrapped in a special boot with a zip, but it was still extremely tender. But none of this dampened Frankie's enthusiasm to be back on board Dubai Millennium at Deauville.

Shortly before he was due to make his comeback at Newmarket, Frankie was preparing Dubai Millennium for the Deauville race. He rode him against a very able horse in Best Of The Bests. The plan was for Best Of The Bests to lead, and for Dubai Millennium to take over in the last stages. At the halfway stage, Dubai

Millennium was still around four lengths down, so Frankie gave him a tap and the champion responded by charging past Best Of The Bests at lightning speed. There was no stopping him, and Frankie was hungrier than ever to get back to business.

Frankie was all set to make his comeback at the July course at Newmarket on Saturday 4 August. Although far from completely fixed, and certainly not in the peak of physical fitness, it was an important step, and one Frankie was keen to take.

That morning, the phone rang, and Frankie received some truly devastating news. Dubai Millennium had fractured a bone in his hind leg that morning whilst out on the gallops. His riding days were over. The best horse Frankie had ever ridden would never be able to race again. Frankie had hit rock bottom.

He was stunned and in a state of complete shock as he walked into the garden where Catherine was playing with Leo. He broke down in tears, inconsolable at the thought that the one thing that had kept him going over those traumatic weeks had been taken from him. He felt like packing it all in there and then, and saw little point in continuing.

But some tough talking from Catherine soon put him straight. She reminded him that so many people had helped him recover from his injuries, and there was no way he could let them down. She also reminded him that people were on their way to Newmarket right at that minute especially to see him ride that afternoon. Frankie knew Catherine was right. He couldn't let his fans down. The only course of action was to pull himself together and get ready for a busy afternoon at Newmarket.

Frankie was greeted by another warm reception of banners and loud cheers as he entered the winner's enclosure before racing that afternoon. The crowd loved seeing their favourite jockey back in action and it was now up to him to give them what they wanted.

He mounted Atlantis Prince and headed for the start, the crowd still cheering him on energetically. As they approached the stalls Frankie turned his head right to the ditch where the plane accident happened just two months earlier. He had to look at the exact spot where it happened, it was an important part of coming to terms with the events of that terrible day. He spared a thought for Patrick Mackey before it was time to get down to the day's business.

With a furlong left, Crazy Larrys took up the running. Then, all the old feelings came back. Frankie was hungrier than ever to win, and he gave Atlantis Prince some encouragement. It worked, as they took the lead and recorded a fairytale victory. More elation from the crowd followed as Frankie made his way back. But the day's work wasn't over yet.

In the next race he rode Dim Sums to victory, giving him a very special double. In the interviews that followed, he dedicated his wins to Catherine, who had done so much to support him in the dark days and weeks that followed the accident.

Frankie was back with a bang, but he was far from completely healed. He felt exhausted after those two races and there was still a long way to go before all his fractures and swellings were healed. He was also reassessing his priorities. He announced he would no longer be riding on Mondays or Tuesdays, in order to spend more time with his family. He also made it clear he would be retiring for good when he reached forty-five, and had no intention of being a jockey in his late fifties as Lester Piggott and Willie Carson had been.

Right now, Frankie is still a long way from forty-five, and only time will tell whether he sticks to that plan, but his idea of not riding on Mondays and Tuesdays hit the buffers within months. There was no way this could be a part-time job – he either has to commit to doing it properly or not at all.

There was always the danger that Frankie was doing too much, too soon, after the accident, and this proved to be the case when York's Ebor meting came around. In the second race of the opening day, Frankie was riding Ski Run when the saddle slipped backwards, leaving Frankie riding bareback for the final three furlongs. This was hard enough in itself, but made all the tougher by the fact Frankie was still nowhere near full fitness and still in considerable pain from his injuries. After one more ride, Frankie called it a day, and didn't return to York for the remaining two days of the meeting. He was trying to do too much and was in urgent need of a break.

He was back to his winning ways by late September, when he won the Fillies' Mile at Ascot on the John Gosden-trained Crystal Music, owned by Andrew Lloyd-Webber, followed shortly afterwards by his first victory in the Cheveley Park Stakes at Newmarket on board Regal Rose, trained by Sir Michael Stoute.

And there was little time to sit back and relax, shortly after Frankie found himself on his way to Canada for the Canadian International Stakes at Woodbine, where he rode Mutafaweq to victory in a Grade 1 race worth over $2 million.

In December, Frankie headed for Hong Kong and he rode Fantastic Light to victory for Godolphin in the $HK 14 Million Hong Kong Cup at Sha Tin racecourse. The horse had run on five different continents and was a deserving winner of the Emirates World Series, and had brought Frankie's season to a triumphant conclusion. Now nobody could doubt he was back, better and stronger than ever.

A year of memorable highs and tragic lows came to a close when Catherine organised a surprise thirtieth birthday party for her husband, shortly before Christmas. She told him they had to attend a charity dinner in Newmarket that evening, which Frankie was reluctant to go to because he was exhausted at the end of a strenuous season, and all he wanted to do was sit at home, eat and drink.

But to please Catherine he grudgingly went along with it. He opened the door at the M club in Newmarket to be greeted by a room full of people singing *Happy Birthday*. Frankie had no idea this was happening, but had an enjoyable evening surrounded by a room full of friends. He was given a large birthday cake in the shape of a Ferrari, which was especially fitting as he'd splashed out £110,000 on a scarlet, two-seater Ferrari Modena during his recuperation, despite promising himself he'd hold on until he reached thirty.

The highlight of the evening came when a Marilyn Monroe lookalike sung a solo to Frankie. It was a fun ending to a poignant year.

The following month it was time to pay tribute to Ray and the extraordinary risks he took in saving Frankie's life and his brave attempt to save the life of Patrick. The Royal Humane Society honoured Ray with a Silver Medal, their top award, which he received from Princess Alexandra in early January.

Later that month at Lester's evening at the Hilton Hotel, he picked up the Special Recognition Award for a flat jockey. Ray Cochrane received a standing ovation from an audience that read like a Who's Who of racing. It was an emotional moment for both Ray and Frankie as they thought back to what they had been through together in the crash the year before. Nobody would argue that he was a worthy recipient of both these honours. He had been totally selfless on that day, putting the wellbeing of Frankie and Patrick before his own.

Before heading off to Dubai, Frankie returned to the Addenbrooke's Hospital in Cambridge with his son Leo to open a new development costing £2.4 million. It also gave him the chance to properly thank those who had helped put him back together six months earlier. Although he was still not completely recovered, he had just had two screws removed from his right ankle leaving him unable to train as vigorously as he would like.

Then, leaving just enough time to be best man at Colin Rate's wedding, it was off to Dubai once more. As always, Frankie was in a rush to get back to full fitness, but this eagerness had some rather unfortunate drawbacks. One day, after Frankie had won a race on Give The Slip, he attempted a flying dismount. As he was about to leap, the horse moved, and because Frankie's ankles weren't yet fully recovered he didn't have enough time to adjust his flight path, causing him to land straight on top of Sheikh Mohammed, who was not amused.

In April, Gianfranco turned sixty and Frankie wanted to take the opportunity to pay tribute to his father from whom he had learnt so much. Yes, it is true Gianfranco was not a perfect father to Frankie as a child, but during the past fifteen years or so he had become a strong, positive influence on his son and was always there for him in times of need. With their differences long healed, they became closer than ever and Frankie wanted to make the most of this opportunity to show his appreciation.

His birthday fell on Liberation Day, 25 April, which is a national holiday in Italy. Celebrations centred around the big race held on that day, the Premio Del Arno, Italy's oldest race. Frankie had planned to celebrate in style. He took Gianfranco to the hotel in a horse-drawn carriage with Frankie controlling the reins. When they arrived, there was a lavish party with three hundred guests. But Frankie had one more big surprise in store.

He took Gianfranco outside to the car park and presented him with his birthday present, a brand new Mercedes. For once, Gianfranco was speechless. He had never been one for the high life, and was truly touched that his son had been so generous towards him. This was certainly light years away from the ice cold, distant figure Frankie had known as a child. Gianfranco was clearly impressed, and wasted no time in fiddling around with the gadgets inside. This was certainly a birthday to remember.

The following day, Frankie managed to win four of his five mounts at Florence, thanks largely to the shrewd booking of rides by Frankie's Italian agent Paolo Benedetti. But as is often the case with Frankie, a wonderful high is often counterpoised with a devastating low, and nothing could have prepared him for the news he received on his return to Britain.

The horse that was taking the world by storm twelve months earlier, Dubai Millennium, was dead. He had contracted grass sickness, a disease that paralyses the intestines, making it impossible to digest food. The Sheikh ensured he received the best possible treatment, and was operated on three times in seven days, and was so strong he stayed alive far longer than anyone had expected. But after the third operation, the Sheikh decided that to make him suffer further was unfair and that he should not come round from the anaesthetic this time. Dubai Millennium's death hit Frankie especially hard. He had achieved so much success in breathtaking style on the horse, and he knew he would be very lucky to ride a horse of his calibre again. Indeed, he'd be lucky to even witness another horse like Dubai Millennium in action during his lifetime.

He died before he had the chance to pass on his talent

at stud. The Sheikh had promised Frankie a nomination to Dubai Millennium, but he couldn't find a suitably priced mare. Now the chance was gone forever. The death hit everyone at Godolphin and it wasn't easy to get on with business for the season after this devastating blow.

Thus the season got off to a slow start, but eventually Frankie made up for lost time thanks to a new star in the shape of Fantastic Light, who clinched the Tattersalls Gold Cup at the Curragh. In the Derby, Frankie had a disappointing race, finishing third on 9-1 show Tobougg, in a race won by Mick Kinane on Galileo.

But once again, he was able to leave Epsom with the valuable consolation prize of the Coronation Cup on Mutafaweq, whom he had rode to victory in Canada at the end of the previous season.

Frankie was optimistic for a fruitful Royal Ascot, which would see him back on Fantastic Light in the Prince of Wales's Stakes. He was drawn on the inside and found himself trapped against the rail with two furlongs left, thanks largely to the efforts of Kieren Fallon. Frankie had no choice but to wait and hope a gap would appear. In the end he held back then came round the outside, taking Fantastic Light sharply left, before charging to the finish and grabbing the race with ease.

Later in the meeting Frankie rode Sheikh Hamdan's two-year-old colt Meshaheer in the Coventry Stakes, a race that, on paper, he was likely to win, but the race turned to disaster. Frankie had a bad draw, which, combined with a poor start, meant the race was doomed fairly early on. He couldn't find his way through the large field and was fortunate to manage third.

The following month Frankie was back at Ascot for what was always going to be a mouth-watering battle between Derby-winning Galileo and Frankie on Fantastic Light in the King George VI and Queen Elizabeth Diamond Stakes. Frankie knew he was going to have a tough battle, especially as he was forced to concede 12 pounds to his rival.

When the race began, Frankie let Mick Kinane track the pacemakers whilst he tucked in behind. Frankie let the race develop but struggled to see a way through the crowd, so decided to switch to the outside. No sooner had he moved position when the pack split leaving Galileo to charge forward, who, of course, had the most direct route round the corner. It seemed that Mick and Galileo had the race all to themselves as they headed down the straight, but Frankie let Fantastic Light go and squared up to Galileo, while Frankie looked Mick straight in the eye, with a furlong left to run. Mick gave Galileo two strikes of the whip, the first striking Frankie hard across the knuckles, badly cutting his hand. Aside from that painful distraction, Frankie had burnt out Fantastic Light moving ground earlier on, so Galileo was duly rewarded for taking the direct route and the race was his by two lengths. The rematch would come in the Irish Champion Stakes at Leopardstown in early September, when Frankie would be hell-bent on revenge for this bitter defeat.

The Glorious Goodwood meeting was a vintage one for Frankie that season, as he secured memorable victories in the Sussex Stakes on Godolphin's three year old, Nouverre, as well as on Sheikh Maktoum's horse Lailani, trained by Ed Dunlop.

Attentions soon turned to the big rematch in Leopardstown. This time, Frankie and Fantastic Light only had to give Galileo 7 pounds. His plan was to sit directly behind Galileo all the way round, then turn inside in the final furlong and beat him on the finish, since Fantastic Light had pace but tended to get idle once in front.

That was the plan, but it was turned upside down the night before the race when Simon Crisford received a phone call from the Sheikh ordering Frankie to fly to Ireland for a summit meeting at the Kildangan Stud.

Frankie arrived late that evening, and took a seat between Sheikh Mohammed and his brother Sheikh Maktoum. His butler offered Frankie a glass of champagne, but Sheikh Maktoum quickly changed the order to a pint of orange juice. This was clearly going to be a serious occasion.

The Sheikhs discussed the tactics Frankie should use on Fantastic Light the following day. As ever, Sheikh Mohammed wanted to employ the bold and ambitious option. He told Frankie he wanted him to jump out in front of Galileo and stay in front of him throughout the race. Frankie protested, since he knew Fantastic Light's one major weakness was his tendency to get lazy when out in front.

The Sheikh was having none of it. His brother agreed that Frankie should go for the bold option. Whether Frankie liked it or not, these were the orders, he was the employee, they owned the horse, and he had to do as they said.

Frankie was convinced they were doing the wrong thing, so he phoned Gianfranco the following morning expressing his concerns. Frankie genuinely believed the race would be lost if he obeyed the Sheikh's instructions. When he arrived at Leopardstown he asked the Sheikh once more if this was what he really wanted. The Sheikh stuck to his guns.

Richard Hills, who rode Godolphin's pacemaker Give The Slip, had agreed to stay off the rail, giving Frankie the option of passing on either side. Frankie chose to pass on the inside, giving him the lead with two furlongs to go. Then Galileo made his presence felt, and Frankie's thoughts turned to Fantastic Light's tendency to ease off when in the lead.

The pair were neck and neck for the next 400 yards, neither giving an inch. Fantastic Light was older and stronger, and seemed hungrier for victory. The Sheikh's tactics were spot on. Fantastic Light had captured a famous victory. We will never know if Frankie would have won if he had been given a free hand to ride as he saw fit, but clearly Sheikh Mohammed wasn't prepared to suffer a repeat performance of the defeat earlier in the year, and his boldness paid off.

Towards the end of August, Frankie won the Juddmonte International at York on Sakhee, leaving runner-up Grandera struggling seven lengths back. The Sheikh had seen enough to enter him for the Arc the following month.

September was a memorable month for Frankie. In

Germany, he rode Kutub in the Preis Von Europa. Kutub had earlier won the Grosser Dallmayr-Preis in Munich and Frankie rode him to a four-length victory over Yavana's pace. He then returned to Ascot for the meeting at which he'd won the seven races five years earlier. The meeting began with the unveiling of a bronze statue of Frankie, a generous gesture, although the statue bears little resemblance to Frankie. A drunk Paul Gascoigne trying to conduct an orchestra maybe, but definitely not Frankie.

Following the unveiling, Frankie rode Fujiyama Crest alongside Jamie Spencer on Decorated Hero along the fronts of the stands. They received an unforgettable reception as everyone recalled their memories of that magical day in 1996. Frankie was in a generous mood, so announced he was giving all his earnings from that day's racing to Barney Curley's charity DAFA to help relieve poverty in Zambia. In the end, Frankie drew a blank that day but donated £10,000 to the cause anyway.

The following weekend, Frankie was in Paris for the Arc. He was in a supremely confident mood as he knew he stood every chance of victory. He told the other jockeys in the sauna early in the day that Sakhee was the real deal and he was going to trounce all of them in the race. They thought he was mad, but Frankie knew he'd look a fool if he messed up after making such a bold prediction. Defeat was not an option.

Sakhee won the race by an incredible six lengths, it became something of a formality without any serious challengers on the soft ground, earning Frankie his 100th Group 1 in the process.

Shortly after, minds became focused on the Breeders' Cup, which left Godolphin with something of a dilemma as to which horse should enter which race. After much deliberation, it was decided Fantastic Light should enter the Turf race over a mile and a half while Sakhee would run in the Classic against Galileo.

The meeting at Belmont Park became all the more poignant as it was the first international sports event in the city since the terrorist attacks of September 11. Frankie and Catherine travelled to Manhattan a few days before the race where they received a warm welcome and were greatly moved by the togetherness and sense of collective grief felt by the people of New York.

Raceday was an emotionally-charged event, which began with a ceremony opened by Carl Dixon, a serving officer in the New York Police Department leading the singing of *Star Spangled Banner*. Just a few miles down the road, his friends and colleagues were still searching through the remains of the twin-towers.

The next part of the ceremony saw many of the leading jockeys, including Frankie, Mick Kinane, Jerry Bailey and Pat Day, hand over their countries' flags to serving police and fire officers. Then it was down to business.

One of Frankie's early rides saw him finish a close second in the Juvenile Fillies. The omens were good when European horses scored notable successes in early races, such as Mick Kinane's victory on the

Juvenile on board Johannesburg. Then came Frankie's turn to shine on Fantastic Light.

Frankie was still aware of the huge question mark that hung over the horse's stamina. He had a good draw and began the race well. Frankie was allowed to trust his instincts this time and held back a little, but the horse was travelling well coming round the bend. Then Frankie let him go and he took four lengths out of the field, before struggling in the final stages. By then, though, he had already done enough to survive a late challenge from Milan, winning by three-quarters of a length.

Next came the chance to ride Sakhee. Just over a furlong out they took a lead from the previous year's winner, Tiznow. Frankie was anxious not to have a repeat of the Swain episode of three years earlier, so maintained a steady rhythm and kept things as simple and methodical as possible. Unfortunately for Frankie, his horse ran out of steam a hundred yards from home and stumbled, sustaining an injury that would cost them the race. Despite soldiering on bravely, Tiznow snatched the race by a nose, cruelly denying Frankie what would have been a memorable double.

But, all in all, it wasn't a bad day's work, with Frankie riding his sixteenth Group 1 winner of the season. There was nothing more Frankie could have done on Sakhee, the injury was not his fault and he was justified in feeling pleased with his day's work. With his season over, Frankie headed for a meal in an Italian restaurant in Long Island with his wife without having to worry about his weight. It had been another good year.

CHAPTER 14

More to Life Than
Being a Jockey

Early in 2002, Frankie headed to Hong Kong to take part in the Macau Derby, which saw him win in convincing style on Royal Treasure. But the victory celebrations were soon muted when they discovered the winning horse's trainer, Allan Tam Man-Chau, known as MC, had been kidnapped by gangsters. He was grabbed in a taxi, beaten up and held to ransom for 10 million Hong Kong dollars. His captors obviously knew he'd had a good day at the office. Luckily it wasn't long before he was rescued by police from a flat in the Macau Peninsula.

Fortunately Frankie had taken a flight home immediately after the race. It was conceivable that they would have captured him, had he stayed on. Later in the spring, he enjoyed further success in Hong Kong – he won the Centenary Sprint cup on Firebolt, trained by Ivan Allen, another man who was lucky to be alive, after being shot several times in Singapore some years earlier.

In the Dubai World Cup, Frankie's loyalty to Sakhee remained paramount, despite him not being in the greatest of shape when being ridden out in the mornings. In the race itself, Street Cry, ridden by Jerry Bailey took the lead in the straight and won convincingly. Sakhee was beaten into third, and it was clear that he hadn't fully recovered from the injury he picked up in New York. He wasn't the same. In fact, he only raced once more before being retired to stud.

Frankie faced a hectic build-up to the 2,000 Guineas that year. He flew out to Louisville to ride Imperial gate in the Kentucky Oaks at Churchill Downs, which took place on the Friday evening. Unfortunately the horse failed to adapt to the heat and ended the race badly dehydrated.

He then hopped on the Sheikh's private jet and headed straight home to ride Naheef in the 2,000 Guineas the following afternoon at Newmarket. He arrived home at seven in the morning, and had just enough time to walk the dogs and head for a sweat in the sauna before going racing. Unfortunately, the race itself turned out to be Frankie's second damp squib in the space of twenty-four hours, as Naheef flopped, preferring trying to bite other horses than race competitively.

The following day came the 1,000 Guineas. Once again, the Sheikh had gone against the judgement of most others involved with Godolphin and entered

Kazzia for the race. Most people believed she'd stand a better chance in some of the less competitive Guineas races in Europe, but the Sheikh was having none of it. He had spotted the horse in action in Germany the previous autumn and bought her soon afterwards. In his mind, he'd invested in a winner and was not going to settle for second best. He wanted top prize and that was that.

Frankie wasn't convinced Kazzia had what it took, so he launched her up with the leaders early on. In the final few furlongs, the others started to catch up, but Kazzia was a strong filly who managed to hold on by a neck, securing the first Classic victory for Godolphin since 1999.

The following Saturday, Frankie was at the Kranji racecourse in Singapore for the Singapore Airlines International Cup. Frankie knew he was in for an awkward ride on Grandera, who had a reputation as a nasty piece of work. There had been an incident in Australia when one of the local vets had tried to take some swabs in the quarantine barn. Grandera charged forward, grabbed his shoulder, dragged him back into the box and had given him one hell of a beating.

Grandera was nasty, yes, but she was also prone to moments of pure genius. After a predictably bumpy ride, Frankie rode him to victory in the race, which held a first prize of £663,000.

Shortly after he returned home, Frankie was hit hard by the news that Mattie Cowing had died. His health had been in decline for some time and he was being kept going by all sorts of medication. In Mattie, Frankie had a firm friend who had stood by him during some of his more difficult periods, as well as being a quite brilliant agent during Frankie's early years as a jockey. He was a walking formbook, and he knew everything there was to know about racing. He was also a true gentleman and all-round family man. He left behind a wife, Rita, and two children, Steve and Julie.

Frankie paid for the reception at the Rutland Hotel following the funeral. After a few drinks, Frankie stood on the table and delivered a heartfelt tribute to his friend and mentor. Everyone there had their favourite story about Mattie, and they gave him a warm and laughter-filled send-off – exactly as he would have wanted it.

The Derby presented something of a dilemma to Frankie, he was torn between Naheef and Moon Ballad. He didn't think Moon Ballad could stay a mile and a half, but he also didn't think Naheef stood much of a chance after his performance in the 2,000 Guineas. In the end he chose Naheef.

But it was another flop for Frankie in the one big race that still eluded him, as Aiden O'Brien's duo High Chaparral and Hawk Wing dominated the race, finishing first and second respectively. Moon Ballad finished third, and Naheef finished way back.

But, as is often the case, Frankie managed to leave Epsom with a valuable consolation prize back on board Kazzia in the fillies' Oaks. They were hit by a downpour early on, but they took the opportunity to get past Kieren Fallon on Islington and held the lead for the remainder of the race, just about holding off a late challenge from Quarter Moon. It was a lucky victory, as Frankie had probably accelerated a bit too early, but Kazzia had proved herself to be a tough battler.

Later in June, Frankie suddenly found himself embroiled in controversy. He was riding the Ed Dunlop-trained Lobos at Newmarket and led for much of the race, before Lobos fell to pieces in the final stages and ended up finishing tenth, which was, horror of all horrors, one place further back than if Frankie hadn't eased up five yards before the line. This happened shortly after the BBC had broadcast a *Panorama* investigation into corruption in racing, and the Jockey Club were especially sensitive to instances such as this as a result.

Local stewards referred the case to the Jockey Club disciplinary committee. They accepted his explanation, but cautioned him for easing the gelding just before the line and warned him about his future conduct. Meanwhile, Ed Dunlop was slapped with a £240 fine for failing to declare that Lobos was lame after the race.

At Royal Ascot, Frankie gave Godolphin their third successive winner in the Prince of Wales's Stakes on Grandera. He settled him down in the middle of the pack, holding him back as he knew there was a very real chance he would grind to a halt if he was to lead. With a furlong to go, he let Grandera charge home, scoring victory by five lengths from Indian Creek.

The Irish Champion Stakes promised to be a thrilling rematch of the previous year's epic between the Godolphin and Aidan O' Brien camps. This time round, Godolphin had two serious contenders in the shape of Grandera and Best Of The Bests, while Aidan lined up the runner-up in the Derby and Coral Eclipse winner, Hawk Wing.

Aidan's horse became odds-on favourite, but Godolphin employed shrewd team tactics to give them every chance in the race. Frankie was eight lengths behind on Grandera two furlongs out, tracking Mick Kinane on Hawk Wing, whilst ahead of them Best Of The Bests closed in on the leader, Sholokhov.

Grandera decided to be as awkward as possible, and when Frankie asked him to quicken he decided he wasn't going to go along with it. By now Hawk Wing was level with Best Of The Bests and the cause seemed lost. Then, he snapped out of his stubborn frame of mind and made up two lengths in fifty yards, and grabbed the race from Hawk Wing by a short head. Frankie had deprived Mick of victory in the race by the shortest of margins for the second year in succession. It was a victory to treasure on the most difficult of horses. For Frankie, this was his fourth victory in the race in five years.

Marienbard had been a low-ranking Godolphin horse the previous season. It was hard to miss him, he was a real giant of a horse, but he had never been considered a true great of the stable. That all changed when Godolphin's trainer, Saeed bin Suroor, persuaded Frankie to do some work on the horse. A year had certainly made a world of difference, and Frankie was instantly impressed by the shape he was in. The condition of the horse was unrecognisable from the slow giant he had known the previous year. During that summer, he was entered for, and won, two big races in Germany: the Deutschland-Preis in Düsseldorf, followed by the Grosser Preis von Baden in late summer at Baden-Baden racecourse.

It was time to test Marienbard in the Arc, something that would have been completely unthinkable just a few months earlier. The race began badly and they were left trailing last in the early stages. Slowly, Frankie weaved his way through the pack and placed himself just behind the leaders. In the straight it was clear High Chaparral was in trouble and Frankie made the most of a gap appearing in front of him, charging into the lead with just a hundred yards left. It was a nail-biting finish, as the French favourite Sulamani gave a late challenge, but Frankie just about managed to hold on to win what would be his last Arc victory to date.

In October, Frankie won the Group 1 Premio Vittorio di Capua in Milan on Slickly for Godolphin for the second year in succession. The same month also saw Frankie make his debut as a team captain on *A Question of Sport*. The decision to accept the invitation to be a regular fixture on the programme was always going to be a tough one. Frankie's days were already pretty full, as staying at the top of his game as a jockey required a disciplined lifestyle and a full calendar for at least nine months of the year. But this opportunity promised to be great fun. Frankie has always been a natural in front of the camera and he fitted all the criteria viewers of the programme had come to expect from a team captain. As a chirpy, quick-witted, and larger-than-life character he followed a long tradition of team captains, including the likes of fellow jockey Willie Carson and the late footballer Emlyn Hughes.

Frankie knew he had a tough act to follow, and his predecessor as team captain, the snooker player John Parrott, had built up a strong rapport with rival captain Ally McCoist that had gone down well with viewers. It would help that the programme had become a much more light-hearted affair than the time Frankie had first appeared in 1990, when much of the banter had been cut out of the recording. And the modern studio set had the audience sat directly behind the teams, allowing Frankie and the other participants to interact and joke with members of the audience from time to time. Frankie was made for the role.

Recording was split between London and Manchester, with three episodes being filmed in one day. He'd usually arrive mid-afternoon, have a cup of tea and a chat with Ally McCoist, record the first show at 4pm, take a short break, record another at 6.30pm and the last one at 9pm. It was always a good laugh, but the days were long and punishing, and added to the pressure his lifestyle brought.

Frankie felt his lifestyle would result in him having a severe disadvantage over Ally on the programme. The reason being, Ally had long since retired from playing and could spend all day watching sport if he wanted, and certainly had the chance to brush up on the guests' achievements. By contrast, Frankie was working long days and just didn't have the time to go into that level of detail.

Although Frankie is a fan of most sports, there are some glaring gaps in his knowledge. He has never got to grips with cricket, for instance, which came across during his time as captain. So he decided to bring two of Colin Rate's friends from Sunderland with him to recording sessions, who would bring him up to speed on his guests' achievements. It helped that his close friend Vinnie Jones was a guest on his first programme, but any nerves were quickly overcome and the producer's instincts were proved correct as Frankie was a complete natural.

Being team captain also gave him the chance to meet many of his heroes from other sports. Michael Owen, in particular, soon became a very close friend and they regularly speak on the phone. The frequent TV exposure outside of racing broadcasts was always going to bring good publicity and would raise his public profile still further.

At the end of the season, Frankie was surprised to be given the opportunity to ride in the Japan Cup on board Falbrav, who had enjoyed a good campaign until disappointing in the Arc, leading Frankie to conclude that he probably wasn't up to the task of winning this race. He got on the phone to Gianfranco, who quickly changed his mind. His father knew Falbrav was a class horse and that the race itself was wide open. Once the sheer unpredictability of the race was pointed out to Frankie, he didn't need much persuading to accept the invitation. So in November, Frankie set off for Nakayama, where the meeting was being held that year while the Tokyo track was being renovated.

The meeting got off to a dream start when Frankie won a double on Cat's Pride and Eagle Café, both trained by his friend, the Japanese jockey turned trainer Futoshi Kojima. The sheer scale of prize money in Japan is mind-boggling. Eagle Café alone earned his owner £700,100 that day.

The following day it was down to the serious business of riding Falbrav. It counted in his favour that the race was a furlong shorter than normal that year due to the change of venue, and when Falbrav managed a solid jump-out at the start, he became a serious contender. He took the tight bends in his stride and charged home in the final furlong. Frankie was still a bit concerned that the distance was a bit much for him at that stage in his career and alarm bells started ringing when Sarfan joined them right on the line resulting in a photo finish.

Frankie was convinced he'd done enough, but so was Corey Nakatani on Sarfan. The result was announced. Frankie had hung on by a nose. Frankie immediately burst into tears, overcome with emotion. He had won the Japan Cup on a horse owned and trained in Italy, and wouldn't have even bothered going there had Gianfranco not worked to change his mind. But his day's work wasn't done. He rode another winner for his friend Futoshi on Precious Café. It was a good day's work, and the long journey to the Land of the Rising Sun had been more than worth it after all.

The year ended with a trip to Cape Town. He managed a few winners during this time, but the trip will be remembered for an entirely different reason –

Frankie was in excruciating pain due to a serious case of piles.

One morning, Peter Burrell went on a desperate search around the township of Soweto for a shop that sold pile cream. But it was only a temporary solution. Frankie managed seven rides on both New Year's Eve and New Year's Day, but after an uncomfortable flight to Cape Town, he felt he could not continue any longer. The local racing authority didn't accept Peter's explanation for Frankie being unable to ride, but that was their tough luck.

Frankie retired to his hotel room with a high temperature, unable to do anything much. This was an occasion when Lester Piggott was seen in a role he had never undertaken before or since, and only had to perform because he had the misfortune to stay in the same hotel as Frankie. The poor guy couldn't have known what he was letting himself in for when he decided to look after his friend Frankie in his hour of need!

Lester was sent to Frankie's room to check on his condition. There was only really one way he could be expected to examine the problem, so Frankie bent over, allowing Lester to take a proper look at the area in question. Lester somehow managed to keep a straight face, before muttering to Frankie that it didn't look nice at all and that he needed proper medical help – and fast!

Shortly afterwards, a retired surgeon made it to Frankie's room. Frankie was paralysed with fright as the surgeon put on a pair of surgical gloves and took the decision to puncture the abscess, which left Frankie rolling around in agony, but had to be done. Frankie needed to get home as quickly as possible to bring this nightmare to an end, and he got the first flight back to Britain just as soon as he was able to travel.

CHAPTER 15

Back Down to Business

Nobody could have guessed just how bad a summer lay ahead for Frankie. He had been in such good form for the previous few years, and it looked like being another strong year ahead with him riding many of the best horses in the world for Godolphin in top class races. After a superb start to the season in Dubai, that is exactly how the season should have panned out. But the moment he started racing on British soil, it all started to fall apart in spectacular, unprecedented fashion, leaving his confidence at an all-time low.

The World Cup meeting in Dubai took place with the war in Iraq going on just a few hundred miles away. Everybody was on edge, fearing for their safety, but as Dubai is a neutral country they were relatively safe, and it was decided that the meeting could go ahead.

World Cup night got off to a dream start as Frankie rode Firebreak to a surprise, but hard-earned victory in the Godolphin Mile. The first big challenge of the evening came on Sulamani in the £750,000 Dubai Sheema Classic. After a good Arc the previous year, the horse had been bought by Godolphin but hadn't impressed the team much leading up to the race.

Then, the day before the race, Sulamani had broken loose and galloped flat out for over three kilometres through the sand dunes with the Sheikh chasing after him in a jeep. Frankie thought the Sheikh was winding him up when he told him the story – how on earth could one of the most valuable horses in the world escape and end up running wild through the desert?

The Sheikh eventually managed to get Sulamani when he tired to a walk. He grabbed him by the tail and held him, before leading him back to the stable completely unharmed. Hardly ideal preparation for a big race!

In light of the previous day's events, Frankie was instructed by the Sheikh not to overdo it on Sulamani, and if he seemed tired, not to burn him out. Frankie began the race by dropping him towards the back. He had pretty much given up hope, when he decided to ease him onto the outside on the straight. With clear ground ahead of him, Frankie gave Sulamani a little gentle encouragement, to which he responded in spectacular style, charging past horse after horse, taking the lead a hundred yards from the finish and claiming an extraordinary victory.

The final challenge of the evening came in the £2.25 million Dubai World Cup. Frankie was faced with a straight choice between riding Moon Ballad and Grandera. It was a tough decision, since both stood a real chance in the race, but in the end he chose Moon Ballad, who had been especially impressive on the gallops.

They got unlucky in being drawn in stall eleven, the widest of all, but Frankie wasn't too distressed by this. He knew Moon Ballad was a classy horse, not quite in the same league as Dubai Millennium, but certainly the best horse taking part in the race. In the end Frankie needed to put in the minimum of effort, winning an incredible five lengths clear of the American, Harlan's Holiday.

Frankie couldn't have asked for a better start, but it was downhill all the way the moment he landed on British soil. His mount Lateen Sails came last in the 2,000 Guineas. It soon became clear that Godolphin's horses weren't as good as they'd hoped for. Frankie had become complacent, and hadn't really bothered to find rides elsewhere, assuming Godolphin would supply him with a healthy array of winners.

His fragile confidence took an enormous knock. Not only was Godolphin out of form, so were other regulars like John Gosden. Frankie could see no way through this barren patch. And things got worse when his relationship with David Loder began to break down. It began when David started to prefer Jamie Spencer over Frankie on his horses.

David was very ambitious and had just broken with Sheikh Mohammed – for whom he had been working solely, concentrating on his two-year-olds – to return to being a public trainer. From David's perspective, it made sense to favour Jamie over Frankie on many occasions, but it didn't help matters when he started playing the two men against each other, increasing pressure on both men to perform well in what became a climate of fear of being dropped completely.

Forcing things never brings the desired results for a jockey, and eventually David snapped, accusing Frankie of not giving his horses a ride in ordinary races. He didn't want Frankie riding his horses in some of the run-of-the-mill races because he felt his heart wasn't in it, so Jamie got the bulk of David's rides.

Frankie was getting stick from every direction, and it began to affect him in a major way. Even so, he was appearing weekly on *A Question of Sport*, doing a few television commercials, and making appearances on chat shows such as *Parkinson* and *Friday Night with Jonathan Ross*.

But what a lot of his detractors didn't realise was that many of these appearances were filmed during the winter months and broadcast months later during the height of the season. It was not as though he was taking days off to film these programmes. Though undoubtedly there were demands on his time outside racing, he was still a jockey first and foremost and many of the criticisms he faced at the time from sections of the media and others in and around the racing fraternity were not entirely justified.

The first signs of improvement came at Royal Ascot, where Frankie rode Dubai Destination to victory for Godolphin in the Queen Anne Stakes. But it was a win in the Irish Oaks the following month that really turned his season around.

BACK DOWN TO BUSINESS

Frankie was booked to ride Vintage Tipple for legendary Irish trainer Paddy Mullins in the race. Paddy was 84 now, and had never won a Classic, but he had trained the great mare Dawn Run who had a young Frankie watching in tears as she won the Cheltenham Gold Cup in 1986.

Paddy didn't say a single word to Frankie in the build-up to the race, leaving all the talking to his son, George, who only passed on a few hints. It was very much up to Frankie how he wanted to play this one. Frankie made a quiet start, placing her behind L'Ancresse, before steering into the lead on the straight, surviving a late challenge from Epsom Oaks winner Casual Looks.

However, it wasn't long before Frankie's confidence faced another threat, which occurred in the most unlikely of settings and came from the most unlikely of people. Frankie was filming for *A Question of Sport* when Thomas Castaignede, the former French rugby fly-half, asked Frankie in total innocence how long he'd been retired. This stung Frankie, as he knew serious questions were being asked about his commitment to riding and it was time to refocus on the day job.

By this time his confidence and self-belief had hit an all time low. During a flight to Deauville in August, he had a long chat with John Gosden about where he was going wrong. John knew Frankie was giving one-hundred per cent, so the problem wasn't with him. If the horses weren't in good shape, that wasn't his fault. So what could it be?

John came to the conclusion that Frankie was putting

himself under enormous pressure by the way he was reacting to his bad run of form. The solution, he suggested, was to get out of his shell and come back as determined as ever, riding flat out every day. The chat with John did Frankie the world of good, but he was to face one more severe setback before things really started to pick up once more.

The following weekend, Sulamani won the Arlington Million in Chicago on the Saturday night. Frankie could have been on board the horse, but Godolphin chose to use local jockey David Flores instead. That hurt in itself, but things were to get a lot worse.

Frankie stayed up late to watch the race, and witnessed Sulamani finish a close second to Storming Home, who threw off his jockey Gary Stevens shortly after crossing the line. At least that's what he thought he saw. So he turned the TV off and went to bed.

The following morning he put teletext on to discover that Sulamani had been given the win after Storming Home was disqualified. It turned out Gary had been thrown off shortly before they crossed the line, leading to disqualification. Later that day at Deauville, people kept coming up to Frankie congratulating him on his win on Sulamani, this shattered his confidence once more.

Later in the month Frankie found himself on the sidelines through suspension, which gave him the chance to take a short break in Sardinia to see Gianfranco. He had always been the one who had been able to get through to his son, having experienced every emotion himself during his years as a multiple champion jockey.

BACK DOWN TO BUSINESS

Gianfranco made it clear that Frankie's selective policy wasn't working and that he had to knuckle down and prove himself again. Gianfranco then took his son to see a guru to help Frankie confront the doubts deep inside him. The solution, they both suggested, was for Frankie to realise he was a champion jockey with the best job in racing and it was time to show he was still the best in the business. A new, positive frame of mind was to emerge from the meeting.

Once back at Newmarket, Colin Rate and Ray Cochrane said pretty much the same thing to Frankie and persuaded him to get back out and ride six days a week once more. Besides, shutting up some of the nastier critics was enough of an incentive in itself by this stage. There were those who said he had so much money by now he didn't care about riding any more, and that he didn't deserve such a cushy job riding world-class horses for Godolphin. It was time to shut them up once and for all.

Early in September, Frankie's new-found frame of mind was starting to pay dividends. He was riding a winner most days, and his old confidence came flooding back when he rode a treble at Lingfield. Suddenly he was winning races all over Europe, picking up the Prix Vermeille on Mezzo Soprano, giving the whole Godolphin team a much-needed boost. Proof that the Godolphin drought was well and truly over came when Mamool won two big races in the space of a month in Germany, winning the Grosser Preis von Baden followed by the Preis von Europa.

It was like he'd never been away. Frankie Dettori was

back, and he was making the racing world sit up and take notice of the man they'd written off as a lazy, part-time jockey just a few weeks earlier. Frankie rounded off a September to remember with victory in the Cheveley Park Stakes at Newmarket on the Jeremy Noseda-trained Carry On Katie.

In November the racing world paid tribute to veteran jockey Pat Eddery, who was retiring after more than thirty years, during which he'd been one of the most reliable men in the business, with only Sir Gordon Richards managing more winners in Britain. Pat's retirement saddened Frankie as he had been someone he'd become very close to over the past few years and had had a profound influence on him, setting a supreme example.

Then, on 13 of November, Frankie silenced his critics once and for all, by recording his first century of winners in a season since 1999, riding Rendezvous Point for John Gosden. He celebrated in style – letting off some steam and spraying champagne over anyone and everyone who got in his way.

During a short break in Dubai, he received a phone call from Luca asking him to ride Falbrav in the Hong Kong Cup. Luca made it clear he'd have preferred Darryll Holland to keep the ride, but the horse's owners insisted on using Frankie. In truth, the horse's owners had wanted Frankie to ride Falbrav all season, but he was never free, which, in turn, allowed Darryll to enjoy a brilliant season on him, which included finishing a close second in the Breeders' Cup Classic.

Once in Hong Kong, Frankie realised Falbrav was in

great shape and stood every chance in the big race. He started the race settling him a fair way back, and the moment he asked the horse to accelerate he charged forward, oozing with unfaltering confidence. From then on, the result was never in any doubt.

Frankie had secured his one-hundred and twenty-first Group 1 win of his career, and celebrated with two flying dismounts, the first when he came back to unsaddle, followed by an extra one for the crowd when they paraded down the course. Suddenly, the misery he'd endured just a few months before seemed a lifetime ago.

This new positive attitude carried on through to the start of 2004. While in Dubai, Frankie rang Ray and they discussed the plan for the season. For the first time in years, Frankie was keen on getting the title of Champion Jockey back. But it was always going to be hard work. By now, Kieren Fallon had won it six times and he was Frankie's biggest threat.

Frankie would have to ride in run-of-the-mill races in smaller racecourses on weekday afternoons and would not be in a position to cherry-pick the best Godolphin rides. He would have to be up and riding out at least four mornings a week, before going on long car journeys up and down the nation's motorways. But Frankie was hungry, and if that's what it took to re-claim supremacy, then so be it.

In February 2004, he made his final appearance as team captain on *A Question of Sport*. From now on, media appearances would come a very distant second to riding.

It wasn't long at all before Frankie's new found dedication paid off. On 7 April, Frankie rode five winners on the card at Folkestone. He picked up victory in the opening race riding Observer, and won the next on board the John Gosden-trained Petite Rose.

Two races later he won on 10-1 shot Wistman, followed by victories on Doctored and Con Horgan's Belle Rouge. He failed to make it six on Zalkani, who slowed down considerably after making the early running. At combined odds of 947-1, it had been a good day for the punter, and a sure sign that Frankie was back, and meant business.

In the 2,000 Guineas, Frankie rode Snow Ridge for Godolphin, who had been purchased from the estate of the late Lord Weinstock. Frankie held back during the early stages as Tumblebrutus led the field, then Richard Hills took the lead on Haafhd and Frankie began his challenge. Unfortunately for Frankie, Haafhd had plenty left in the tank and he was forced to settle for second place.

But Frankie's season was put on hold after he was sidelined through injury following a freak accident at Goodwood. Shortly before the start of the Mitsubishi Diamond Vision Handicap, a pheasant flew out of a tree, spooking Frankie's mount Chinkara on the way to post. The horse whipped round to the left, catching Frankie's hand and fracturing a bone in the process.

In the Derby, Frankie was back on board Snow Ridge for Godolphin. Despite the disappointment of the 2,000 Guineas, this looked like being Frankie's best ever chance in the Derby, and many felt Snow Ridge would benefit from the slightly longer race. Frankie was more optimistic than ever before of clinching victory this time round. The bookies agreed, making Snow Ridge 7-2 joint favourite. But yet again, the race brought disappointment.

Despite a solid start that saw Frankie tucked just behind the leading bunch, he soon found himself boxed in on the inside rail. In the home straight, he moved over to the outside and began a surge that looked threatening at one point, but in the final furlong Snow Ridge ran out of steam leaving Keiren Fallon on North Light to hold on for a commanding victory.

Afterwards, there was no disguising Frankie's disappointment. He had ridden in twelve Derby's, but had failed to make a serious impact in any of them. He took solace from the fact Sir Gordon Richards didn't win his first Derby until he was 49, but there was no denying the fact this was a golden opportunity lost. Although Frankie had probably done the right thing moving Snow Ridge to the outside, the horse just didn't have the pace to hold out in the final furlong, finishing a distant seventh.

But despite the disappointment of the Derby, Frankie's bread-and-butter racing was going from strength to strength. For the first time in years, Kieren Fallon wasn't having it all his own way in the table as a determined Frankie showed the same level of ambition to gain the title he had had ten years previously.

With this unrelenting determination, Frankie was likely to be in for a memorable Royal Ascot. The meeting got off to a thrilling start as Frankie rode Refuse To Bend in the Queen Anne Stakes. In the final furlong, he was involved in a tense battle against Johnny Murtagh on Soviet Song. Frankie's horse had been out of form since the previous year's 2,000 Guineas victory, but the horse showed a gritty determination and accelerated strongly in the final stages, holding on by a neck to get Frankie's Royal Ascot off to the best possible start.

In the Ascot Gold Cup, Frankie was down to ride Papineau, the colt of Singspiel on whom Frankie had won the Coronation Cup in 1996. The Sheikh had warned Frankie not to let go too soon as he had done on an earlier ride at Sandown, and with that in mind Frankie had a good chance of claiming his fourth Gold Cup victory.

Frankie's confidence was on a high going into the race, having won the previous race of the afternoon on Punctilious. Everything was going according to plan. He held back in the early stages, frustrated at being unable to find a gap, as the Japanese raider Ingrandine made the early running, before guiding Papineau into a good position with five furlongs to go.

He got in behind French jockey Gerald Mosse on Westerner, as they broke away from the pack with two furlongs remaining. Then, Frankie asked Punctilious to go on a charge and took the lead on the inside, making the race look easy by winning by a length-and-a-half.

In July, Frankie was back on board Refuse To Bend in the Eclipse Stakes at Sandown. The horse had had a disappointing start to the season after winning the 2,000 Guineas so memorably the previous year. A hugely disappointing run in Dubai in March followed by an equally disappointing performance at Newbury's Lockinge Stakes two months later led many to suspect his best days were behind him. Yet that win at Royal Ascot had shown in memorable style that all was not lost and that the horse was in with a very real chance in this race.

Yet Refuse To Bend was unproven over ten furlongs, so this was never going to be an easy ride. In the final few furlongs, Frankie thought his opportunities to break had gone, and believed that kicking out now would be too big a test of stamina, but he needed to do something to stand any chance of winning. He decided to take a chance and break out, taking the lead in the final furlong over Warrsan, who in turn responded by increasing the pace in the final moments of the race. But Frankie had done enough, and timed the charge to perfection, just holding out for victory. Another big race was in the bag. The season was going from strength to strength.

Later that month Frankie rode Doyen to victory in the King George VI and Queen Elizabeth Diamond Stakes at Ascot, in what proved an eventful day. Firstly came a nasty fall as he approached the stalls on the restless two-year-old Nightfall, sending him flying through the air before crashing to the ground. Frankie must have been practicing falling safely, as he only suffered a few bruises and was declared fit to ride in the race.

He jumped out sharply and took command of the race early on. In the final furlong they managed to see off a late challenge from Moth Ball who appeared on the inside from nowhere. Frankie managed to get the best out of the sprightly, youthful colt and just about held on for another victory, sealing Frankie's two-thousandth winner in the process. There was no hiding his delight on the way back, as he held two fingers in the air to signify his dual-millennium before performing a flying dismount with extra panache.

However, the celebrations had to be put on hold until he had ridden Doyen four races later. In the big race, Frankie and Doyen held out for victory over Gary Stevens on the American raider Hard Buck, declaring it the easiest King George winner he had ever ridden.

Frankie's confidence is notoriously fragile, as had been shown by his state of mind the previous season. But now, he was unstoppable, his fears must have seemed a lifetime ago.

The following month in the Juddmonte International, Frankie was back on board Sulamani. Once Norse Dancer had run out of steam in the closing stages, they took the lead and managed to win by three-quarters-of-a-length. Finally, Sulamani had impressed on British soil. After winning three Group 1 races abroad in the previous twelve months, he had never got the credit he'd deserved in the British press. It was time to sit up and take notice – there was still plenty left in the tank.

10 October 2004 was the day it became clear the title of Champion Jockey would be heading in Frankie's direction. The meeting at Leicester brought Frankie a treble, extending his lead over Kieren Fallon to 13. Frankie knew the title was in the bag later that day when Kieren sustained what appeared to be a nasty fall. Though the fall was nowhere near as bad as initially thought, even a short spell on the sidelines

meant that Kieren's chances of catching Frankie had been reduced to nil. Kieren's years of dominance were over, and Frankie was Champion Jockey once more.

Frankie received some unfair criticism in the days that followed, with some arguing that Frankie's success came on the back of Kieren's troubles. Yes, this had been a season riddled by injury for Kieren, and this was around the time allegations of race-fixing by Kieren began to surface, which came as another unhelpful distraction to his season, but Ray was having none of it. There was no doubt in his mind that Frankie won the title on merit, chalking up 192 winners, a higher tally than on two of Kieren's Championship-winning years. Ray pointed out that even if Kieren hadn't sustained injuries, the title would still have gone Frankie's way because Godolphin's stable had been so strong all year, and Frankie's level of determination and enthusiasm for riding had been higher than for many, many years.

Frankie's season continued apace with a trip to Canada, where he was to ride Sulamani in his final race before retiring to stud in the Canadian International at Woodbine. Frankie began the race quietly, allowing Burst Of Fire to make the initial running, tucking Sulamani away on the inside, which left him needing to make up seven lengths with three furlongs to go. It was a case of holding on and waiting for an opportunity to present itself. Then, a gap appeared in the straight when Kieren's horse Simonas kicked, so, spotting the gap, Frankie switched wide to make his challenge, taking the lead half-way inside the final furlong before taking the race.

Frankie enjoyed further international success in October, taking the Prix De L'Abbaye De Longchamp on the Clive Brittain-trained Var.

A ban imposed by Australian stewards for careless riding in the Melbourne Cup left Frankie on the sidelines for most of November and early December, before ending the year by taking part in the Hong Kong Mile on board Firebreak for Godolphin. After finishing a disappointing fifth the previous year, he had largely been written off by everyone apart from those close to Godolphin, who knew his potential and realised he was worth another try, having picked up the Godolphin mile in the past two years.

Frankie had the five-year-old Charnwood Forest horse handily placed from the start, racing initially in fourth and then third. Then, two furlongs out, Frankie switched to the outside and charged past leader Scintillation, before clinching the race with supreme confidence by three quarters of a length from Perfect Partner, earning Godolphin their eleventh Group 1 winner of the year.

By the end of 2004 Frankie had well and truly silenced those who had considered him a part-time jockey the previous year. With renewed dedication, and far fewer outside distractions, Frankie meant business, and he had fired a warning shot to his rivals all around the world that he was far from finished. He had proved himself in emphatic, unforgettable style. Nobody would dare write him off as a full-time celebrity and a has-been, part-time jockey again. Frankie had earned the last laugh.

CHAPTER 16

Getting Through Tough Times

At the beginning of 2005, it seemed as though Frankie and Godolphin could do no wrong. All the doubts about the level of Frankie's dedication had been answered, he was champion jockey, riding winners wherever he went, and there seemed nothing that would stop him being at the very least a serious contender for the title of Champion Jockey in the year ahead.

For Godolphin, too, there was a spirit of supreme optimism at Al Quoz at the start of the year. There was a promising crop of three year old colts who threatened to dominate the scene in the year ahead, such as Dubawi, Belenus and Shamardal, a son of Giant's Causeway and winner of the previous year's most prestigious juvenile race, the Dewhurst.

They were also in hot pursuit of the next Dubai

Millennium. Five of his sons, Dubawi, Belenus, Echo of Light, Oude and Rajwa, and two of his daughters, Kydd Gloves and Halle Bop, were among those gliding over the Al Quoz track at the start of the year.

It seemed as though Frankie and Godolphin were ready to take on the world. Sadly, over the course of the season, it seemed as though anything that could go wrong did. They were about to be hit by an unrelenting run of bad luck.

It began right at the start of the season in the build up to the Dubai World Cup. Frankie was due to ride Grand Hombre in the race. The horse had finished fourth the previous year and now looked like being a serious contender for the big prize. But just a few days before the race, Grand Hombre suffered a stone bruise during work and had to be pulled out.

Frankie found himself a very able substitute in Shamardal, who started the race as favourite, but the horse had never run on dirt before and failed to cope with the experience of having sand kicked in his face, fading tamely in the straight in a race won by Martin Dwyer on the Andrew Balding-trained Phoenix Reach.

It was a sign of things to come. In the 2,000 Guineas, Frankie was on board Dubawi, whom many within the Godolphin team were expecting to follow in his father's footsteps. He had wintered well, and went into the race favourite.

The race went according to plan until the final furlong when Dubawi failed to respond to Frankie's attempts to quicken up, veering left before finishing a disappointing fifth. The race was won by

Footstepsinthesand ridden by Kieren, who had fired a warning shot firmly in Frankie's direction, telling him that he was not going to have it all his own way this season and that he was hungry to get his crown back.

A month later at The Curragh it was time to make amends for the disappointment in the Irish 2,000 Guineas. The Sheikh's instincts, so often correct in the past, told him Dubawi was something special. He made no secret of his faith in the horse in the build-up to the race, telling the doubting press, 'He is a champion. We knew he was a champion, but at Newmarket something went wrong. Now he is back. He is just like you or me, flesh and blood. Something can always go wrong.'

Frankie broke well before settling into fourth place, where they maintained a steady pace during the early stages. Then, in the straight, he cruised up to the leaders and took the lead two furlongs out. He crossed over to the far rail and ran on strongly to go clear before being eased down. It was an emphatic victory, leaving Kieren and his horse, Oratorio, trailing way back.

A week earlier Frankie had claimed the French 2,000 Guineas on Shamardal. It looked as though his season was finally taking off. However, at the end of the month Frankie was handed a six-day ban for careless riding that would see him miss the entire Royal Ascot meeting, held at York while Ascot was being redeveloped. It happened when he was riding Royal Orissa in a race at Haydock. The horse appeared to make a manoeuvre right which resulted in Aversham taking a crashing fall, sending jockey Fran Berry crashing to the ground.

Fortunately both horse and jockey escaped unscathed, and Frankie decided not to appeal against the ban, describing it as a freak accident that happens from time to time. However, there was no hiding the disappointment of missing the whole of the most prestigious meeting of the year. But for now, he had to put his disappointment to the back of his mind and focus all his energies on trying to win the Derby on the ominous thirteenth attempt.

The Epsom meeting began well. Frankie won the opening race, the Princess Elizabeth Stakes, on Sundrop. In the big race, Frankie was back on Dubawi. This was as good a chance as Frankie had ever had in the big race. Would this be the year he finally broke the curse that had haunted him for so long?

The race began according to plan as Frankie settled Dubawi in mid-division and moved him up on the turn into the straight and soon went third and then second on the run to the line. But Johnny Murtagh on Motivator then went clear of the field and Walk In The Park finished a convincing second, leaving Frankie and Dubawi a disappointing third. It seems Dubawi just ran out of steam at the crucial time.

Godolphin trainer Saeed bin Suroor was philosophical about the defeat, and said that the race had taught him that a mile to a mile-and-a-quarter was the best distance for him. But for Frankie, this seemed like another golden opportunity lost. His confidence hit another low. The setbacks in the big races, and the ban had all taken their toll, and Frankie's tally in the smaller races was far from impressive.

The following day at the French Derby, Frankie was back on Shamardal, hell-bent on revenge after the disappointment of the previous day. This time both Frankie and Shamardal were on top of their game and there was no stopping them.

He broke cleanly from the stalls and soon went ahead on the outside before gradually tracking over to the rail. Frankie slowed the pace down, knowing that there was still a long way to go and it was crucial to have a bit left in the tank for the closing stages.

Turning into the straight, Frankie established a two length advantage before accelerating two furlongs out. The horse's stamina had run out in the final hundred yards, but it barely mattered, the hard work was done. Odds-on favourite Hurricane Run's late charge was too little, too late. Frankie had done his homework and rode Shamardal to perfection.

At the end of June Frankie's confidence received another much-needed lift as he won the Grand Prix de Saint-Cloud for the first time, riding five-year old Alkaased for Luca. The horse had been the runner up in the Coronation Cup at Epsom, but this race was always going to be a tough ask with the previous year's Arc winner, Bago, in the field. In the end, Frankie made the race look easy as Bago struggled to get going, only managing to make up ground when it was too late to finish third. Meanwhile Yeats, the horse that had beaten Alkaased in the Coronation Cup, struggled back in a distant second. Finally Frankie seemed back to his old self, winning major races in quick succession while his tally in ordinary races was starting to improve to something like the level of the previous year.

But more misery was around the corner at the beginning of July when he broke his left collarbone in a heavy fall at Sandown that would leave him on the sideline for many weeks. He was hurled to the ground when his mount, Celtic Mill, lost his footing with a furlong to go.

A long lay-off was inevitable, and he was only able to return to action in the final week of August. All thoughts of retaining the Jockey's title were long gone. There had simply been too much bad luck during the season to catch the leaders Jamie Spencer and Seb Saunders, and he could only watch from the sidelines as Dubawi won the Prix Jacques le Marois at Deauville.

When the day of the comeback finally arrived, it couldn't have gone any worse for Frankie. He arrived at Newmarket at midday, and was in the weighing room long before anyone else arrived. It felt good to be back, but the day was to bring nothing but disappointment. In his first race he trailed home in tenth on Princess Bada. Undeterred, he gave a thumbs-up to the crowd on his way back, it just felt good to be back in the saddle after such a long lay-off.

However, further disappointment would follow before the day was out. His next ride, Melodic Score, was never challenging, and he also failed to trouble the frame aboard Bayeux and The Jobber.

It wasn't until the St Leger that Frankie really got back to his brilliant best, riding Scorpion, trained by Aidan O'Brien and owned by John Magnier and

Michael Tabor – the only people in racing powerful enough to regularly take on the Sheikh. Frankie took Scorpion straight to the head of the six runners once they had stumbled out of the stalls, with 14 gruelling, soggy furlongs ahead of them. Throughout the race he steadily increased the pace, seeing off the likes of Hard Top and eventual runner-up The Geezer to win the race in rugged, inelegant yet highly effective style.

However, massive controversy was to follow in the weeks ahead. It turned out that Godolphin had released Frankie on St Leger day to ride Motivator in the Irish Champion Stakes and not Scorpion for John Magnier and his partners. Frankie took the mount on Scorpion when it looked likely that fast ground would rule Motivator out of the Irish race, a decision that clearly did not go down well with the Sheikh.

A few weeks later Frankie and Aiden O'Brien had a massive falling out. Jockey Seamus Heffernan was banned after the Queen Elizabeth II Stakes at Ascot for his riding of Ivan Denisovich. Frankie, riding Librettist for Godolphin, had accused Heffernan of taking him wide round the home turn to help the eventual winner, George Washington, and the Ascot stewards on the day agreed with him.

Aiden accused Frankie of, 'Throwing the toys out of his pram' by reporting Seamus to the stewards at Ascot that day. Seamus appealed against his 14-day ban for 'team tactics', an accusation that was later downgraded to 'improper riding'. Aiden continued his tirade against Frankie saying, 'He's either paranoid about Ballydoyle horses or he knew he'd given his horse such a bad ride he wanted a way to cover himself. Our horse got taken out twice and it's the most absurd thing I've seen in my life. He caused it and everyone believed him.'

Bu the stewards did not find Dettori had given his horse a bad ride, nor did they find Frankie had taken out Hefferman's horse. And this was just the latest episode in an increasingly bitter row between racing's two big superpowers. In the end the Sheikh banned Frankie from riding any horses connected to Magnier in future. Although Frankie tried to stay out of the feud as much as possible, he clearly upset the Sheikh on that day and the pressure surrounding the row had taken its toll and had been an unwelcome distraction from the business of riding, with Frankie's only major win for Godolphin for the rest of the season coming on Cherry Mix in the Gran Premio del Jockey Club in Milan in October.

Frankie ended the domestic season with a disappointing tally of just 87 winners, leaving him trailing way back in fifteenth in the table. A mixture of bad luck with injury and suspensions, combined with an earlier out-of-form but soon recovered Godolphin operation, as well as an unpleasant atmosphere caused by racing politics helped make this the most disappointing of seasons.

There was, however, one more opportunity to end the season on a high. In November, Frankie was down to ride Alkaased for Luca in the Japan Cup. With Luca well removed from the politics surrounding racing at the time, Frankie could spend his time in Japan focussing on what he does best. He had an unlucky draw, in stall 14, so from the outset moved sharply across, well aware that Alkaased's only weakness was that he was a slow starter. He overpowered his rivals in the home straight before holding off a late surge by Heart's Cry to win the race by the narrowest of margins in a photo finish that took several minutes to be declared. Shortly afterwards, Alkaased was sold to the Sheikh's Darley operation.

As usual, Frankie ended the year in Hong Kong, but failed to make an impact at Sha Tin this time. However, it wasn't the racing that the British contingent at Sha Tin will remember Frankie for during the trip. The journey back from the course is notoriously difficulty because of the sheer number of people trying to get out at once, making a long wait in the traffic inevitable. Frankie left the course with a coachload of distinguished guests. It looked like being another long, boring journey until Frankie decided to take to the microphone. He performed an impromptu cabaret act, taking the mickey out of his distinguished fellow passengers, including trainer Sir Michael Stoute, racing manager Angus Gold, and even noble Lord Derby himself. The act was sharp, cutting and irreverent, and Frankie didn't allow knighthoods and peerages to deter him from poking fun at virtually everyone on board. But it was all good-humoured and highly entertaining, and brightened up what looked like being another dreary journey away from Sha Tin.

There was no hiding the fact that this had been a disappointing year. He had only ridden seven Group 1 winners, a good year by the standards of most, but by now he was used to winning ten or more. He ended the year by taking his family to Disneyland in Orlando over Christmas, before preparing to have another stab at retaining the jockeys' title in 2006.

The year began as always with the Dubai World Cup in March which saw Frankie on board Electrocutionist, who had won the previous year's Juddmonte International with Mick Kinane on board, and had been seen as one of Godolphin's most promising horses after they bought him from Earle Mack. They had a poor draw in stall one tight against the rail, and, after a poor start, looked like being a dead loss. But Frankie switched his mount superbly with six furlongs to go and once he accelerated, he was in control and overhauled his rivals close to home, seeing off the American hope Brass Hat inside the final furlong, winning the race by a length and a half.

Yet despite this great start to the season, it would be several months before either Frankie or Godolphin picked up another major race. Simon Crisford played down Godolphin's chances in the 2,000 Guineas, claiming Frankie's ride, the 12-1 shot Opera Cape was unlikely to make much of an impact in the race. On the day, Frankie was unable to make any kind of progress on the horse and Godolphin's best horse in the race was Olympian Odyssey ridden by reigning champion jockey Jamie Spencer.

Frankie's fourteenth attempt at the Derby proved yet another major disappointment as he rode French trainer Andre Fabre's horse Linda's Lad in the absence of a major Godolphin contender. The horse had been reluctant to go to the start and despite Frankie's best efforts to get him going, he never looked like making much of an impact. The biggest race of all still continued to allude him.

The lack of major rides for Godolphin continued through to Royal Ascot, where Frankie failed to win a major race. It was clear by now that Frankie was not going to be a contender for the title of champion jockey for another year, with such a disappointing crop for the big early season races,. Though the disappointing crop was unrelated to Godolphin's continuing bitter feud with Ballydoyle, the row remained an unwelcome distraction from racing.

Frankie finally managed to win an important Group 1 race on board the Ed Dunlop-trained Ouija Board, owned by the Earl of Derby, in the Nassau Stakes at Glorious Goodwood. Welcome though this was, Godolphin were not making their presence felt in the major races and Simon's early season prediction had proved all too accurate.

The season began to turn in August when Frankie rode Librettist for Godolphin in the Prix Jacques le Marois at Deauville. Frankie settled the horse in fourth place early in the race and travelled consistently before they moved up the field around three furlongs out. Then, with a furlong and a half to go, Frankie kicked for home holding on for victory by a neck.

In the final week of August, thieves broke into Frankie's home, stealing his MBE award along with the three Gold Cups he had won in Japan. Frankie discovered the burglary after returning home from

Salisbury after a day's racing, leaving him feeling deflated and sickened. At the time of writing, they have not been returned, though the police are optimistic that they will turn up, due to the large amount of publicity the case has received, making the stolen goods difficult to sell on. That said, this was clearly not a random burglary – they could have stolen any number of trophies or expensive electronic equipment from Frankie's home, so they clearly knew what they were looking for.

St Leger day began with the devastating news that Electrocutionist had died of a heart attack during the night. The news rocked the entire Godolphin operation, not least Frankie himself who had been expecting many more big winners on the promising horse. There was little time to dwell on this, however, as later in the day he would be riding hot favourite Sixties Icon in the big race. The Last Drop, a 50-1 outsider, hit the front with two furlongs to travel, but Frankie was just biding his time and he burst clear with a furlong to go. He won by two-and-a-half lengths from The Last Drop, who stayed on to finish second, with Red Rocks in third. The win gave trainer Jeremy Noseda his first Classic victory, and Frankie his hundredth winner of the season.

Early in September, Frankie was back on board Librettist in the Prix du Moulin de Longchamp. After a good break from the stalls, Frankie and Librettist took up the running and dictated the pace all the way round, quickening up at the beginning of the straight. They held off late challenges from Stormy River and

Manduro to win by half a length, giving Librettist his fifth win of the season.

In October, Frankie enjoyed a memorable Arc meeting, winning his first Prix du Cadran on the Rod Millman-trained Sergeant Cecil, as well as winning his first Prix de la Foret on Caradak for Godolphin. Frankie got off to a clean start, settling the horse in the middle of the pack before moving to the outside to go fourth. A strong run in the final furlong saw them charge into the lead, holding on for victory by a short neck.

Frankie rode his last major winner of the year on board Lord Derby's brilliant mare Ouija Board in the Breeders' Cup Filly and Mare Turf at Churchill Downs, a race the horse had won two years earlier with Kieren Fallon riding. During the race, Frankie broke well before moving up from fourth on the bend and charging past Film Maker and Honey Rider to give the horse an incredible two wins in three years, and trainer Ed Dunlop an important win after breaking free from Sheikh Maktoum's Gainsborough operation. Talk of Frankie's nightmare on Swain back in 1998 was now banished for good. This was a classy victory, and the crowd and media vultures knew it.

Shortly afterwards, Ouija Board became the first horse in the 16-year history of the Cartier Awards to win the award for a second time.

Frankie rounded off a memorable trip to America with victory in the Breeders' Cup Turf on an unfancied long-shot called Red Rocks, based in Ireland and trained by Brian Meehan. Despite having never finished lower than third in his previous outings, he was never considered a serious threat to the favourites in the big race. Inevitably, Frankie had memories of his disaster on Swain years earlier in the back of his mind, despite having won the race in breathtaking style on two occasions since. They started near the back of the pack, allowing the favourites to tire themselves out as they fought one another early on. As the frantic pace slowed down, Frankie guided Red Rocks to the outside, and charged down, taking the lead with plenty left in the tank. Frankie had timed it to perfection, which was just as well as Ramon Dominguez on Better Talk Now was playing a similar waiting game to Frankie and mounted a late charge. Frankie's precision finally paid off and the race was in the bag.

Once again, Frankie had proved the depth of his skills as a jockey on the biggest stage in the world. If there were still any critics left who wanted to talk about Swain, they had surely been silenced for good after he had managed to win two Breeders' Cup races in one day, becoming the first European jockey to ride a double at the meeting in the process. Frankie was already on the plane to Australia when it was announced he had received the Bill Shoemaker Award for the outstanding riding performance at the 2006 Breeders' Cup. Although he wasn't there to collect the award in person, it inevitably took pride of place on his mantelpiece, not only because of his heroic achievements at the meeting, but because the award was named after one of his all-time heroes, who is sadly no longer with us.

Frankie soon found himself back on Ouija Board in

the Japan Cup. His instructions were to hold on for as long as possible, but ultimately the plan did not work as Deep Impact put in an incredible performance, sailing down the outside to win, leaving Frankie and Ouija Board trailing in third behind Dream Passport. There were no excuses – the tactics hadn't paid off and Deep Impact had been supremely impressive on the day.

Frankie was hoping to sign off his season by riding Ouija Board to her second victory in succession in the Hong Kong Vase, signing off her spectacular career that had brought no fewer than seventeen Group 1 winners in style. However, the day before the race, this dream was cruelly shattered when the mare was found to be lame during a routine examination. She had jarred herself either on the dirt or the grass and there was a risk of further damage if she had been allowed to run. It was a sad end to an illustrious career, and a disappointing way for Frankie to end a season which had seen him overcome the disappointment of a poor crop of horses from the Godolphin stable early on and go on to prove he is still the greatest jockey in the world by winning major races in three continents during the course of the season.

CHAPTER 17

Life After Riding

The plane crash of 2000 undoubtedly had a profound effect on Frankie and his outlook on life. Riding was put into perspective and he realised that it did not mean nearly as much to him as his wife and children. He soon came to a firm decision – he would give riding ten more years, then retire for good at the age of 40, though he has subsequently said he will continue until he reaches 45. The buzz and determination was still there, but he discovered that there was more to life than playing this exhausting, dangerous game to please the punters.

It wasn't long before Frankie began making preparations for life after riding. Riding The Magnificent Seven had massively elevated his celebrity status, which had remained consistently high during the years since. Without trivialising the plane crash, the way in which he had dealt with these harrowing events had only enhanced the affection by which he is held by the British public.

By now, he had lent his name to a number of commercial endorsements, and decided the time had come to begin a business venture of his own. As is often the case with highly successful sports stars, the brand name they create outlives their careers as sportsmen. For example, the Fred Perry clothing range continues to flourish long after his retirement and death. The same can be said for the way 'Brand Beckham' is arguably now more valuable than Beckham the footballer. With a flamboyant and likeable personality, popular with the British public, the Dettori brand looks set to outlive Dettori the jockey.

Being Italian, and having been brought up on traditional Italian home cooking, the food industry seemed a natural choice. Frankie had been talking about launching a food range for a long time, but it took the plane crash for him to finally do something about it. However, due to his discerning nature on culinary matters, it would take more than a year before the product range was finally ready for launch.

He began drawing up plans over lunch with a neighbour, who was already heavily involved with the market. From the outset, Frankie was very specific in his demands. He wanted to go into the frozen pizza market, but these were not to be any old pizzas. He made it clear that he found many of the frozen pizzas generally available were sub-standard and cardboard-tasting and that his range was only to be made from the highest quality ingredients. Though a noble motive, this was ultimately to contribute to the downfall of the range.

He spent a whole year sourcing the best products; no compromises were made on the quality of ingredients. Then a range was developed. The old favourites were there, albeit with an upmarket twist, but the range also included less well-known delicacies such as the garlic pizza. To this was added the pasta sauce range, and finally the ice cream range, which included such flavours as Zabaglione, Caffe Latte and Apricot Amore. The range donned the colours of the Italian national flag and were all graced with Frankie's face gurning coyly from the packaging. Frankie Dettori Italian Foods Ltd was up and running.

Hindsight is a wonderful thing, no more so than in business, where it is always easy to look back at where past mistakes have been made and kick yourself for making them. But in Frankie's case it appears some errors were made in the promotion and distribution of the brand.

The Dettori range was launched in January 2002, with the selling rights given to Iceland and Sainsbury's, both of whom were going through a difficult period at the time, and would see major restructuring over the next few years.

Few would argue that Dettori's pizzas were the best quality product on the market at the time, but their downfall was the price. There was very little difference between the price of a Dettori's pizza and the cost of eating a pizza in a restaurant. Most people, it seems, decided it simply wasn't worth the money. Iceland's interior newsletter mentioned a range of Dettori ice cream the following June, but it could not be found at all in large sections of the country.

Peter Burrell, Frankie's business partner, openly admits he found dealing with the supermarkets a frustrating and highly irritating experience, with chief executives moving from one firm to another, and lengthy delays caused by a whole range of problems.

Shortly before Christmas that year the Frankie Dettori ice cream range appeared in Tesco. Again, the range was upmarket and could be described as reassuringly expensive. This was top of the range produce and had some excellent reviews, but it never really took off. Within a year, the pizza and ice cream range had disappeared from the shelves. Peter is certainly in no rush to give a frozen food range another go.

The only surviving remnants of the Dettori food range are the tinned tomatoes and tinned kidney beans. Again, these are upmarket products canned in factories with their own fresh supply from fields in the regions of Puglia, Campania, Lazio and Toscana, before being prepared and packaged in Italy. They have a fresher flavour than most of their market rivals, and have sold consistently well since the launch, but can now only be found on shelves in Morrisons supermarkets.

A far more successful business venture came in the form of Frankie's ever-expanding restaurant empire. One evening, Frankie popped into Drone's restaurant for a meal and got chatting with renowned fiery chef Marco Pierre White, the youngest chef ever to get three Michelin stars, but who is probably best known to the majority of the British public as the man who trained Gordon Ramsay, and famously made him cry.

They got talking about London restaurants and the lack of family-style restaurants in the city that catered for all age groups. Then Frankie had a brainwave – he wanted to create a dining experience for the whole family, combined with a touch of glamour where parents can enjoy a decent bottle of wine while the children can be themselves. In other words, Frankie wanted to bring Italian-style family dining to Britain.

As always, Frankie insisted on having a reasonable amount of input into the creative side of things, and a menu was devised offering a range of pasta, pizza and burgers, as well as an extensive wine list.

The first Frankie's Italian Bar and Grill opened in Knightsbridge, with others following in Chiswick, Oxford Street and Putney. In 2007, the chain is expected to expand to new territories. In March, a 200-seater restaurant was opened in Dubai, with a 250-seater branch opening in Shanghai the following month.

Over the past few years, Frankie has also been looking to launch a line of men's skin and beauty products. In 2005, he entered into discussions with KLW, a health and beauty company headed by Ken Wells, a former commercial director at cosmetics firm, Coty, about developing a range to be branded 'Flying Jockey', with distribution rights going to Asda and Boots stores. However, this attempt has been put on the back burner for a time, although Frankie is still set to launch his own range, which will be available in duty free stores in the Emirates.

ARISE SIR FRANKIE DETTORI

The success of the restaurants and the ambitious plans to expand the empire prove Frankie is a shrewd businessman. He spotted a gap in the market and brought a new and popular style of eating to Britain, and he has ambitious plans to expand still further. It seems likely there will be other attempts to capitalise on the popularity he enjoys with the British public, which look set to keep his name, and his face, in the public eye long after he retires from the saddle.

But when will that retirement come? Who knows? He said he would retire when he hits 40 in an interview shortly after the terrible plane crash. Yet, in 2006, he told Sue Lawley on Desert Island Discs that he would retire when he's 45. He has made it clear he has no intention of continuing riding to a grand old age, as Lester Piggott and Pat Eddery did. Maybe he doesn't want the ever-more difficult pressure of keeping his weight down hanging over him forever.

But then again, as he would be the first to admit, nothing will ever give him a buzz like riding winners does. Once he's retired, nothing will ever replace it. Perhaps the most pressing issue is whether there is anything left for him to achieve in racing. He has stated that he'd like to win the Derby on one of the Sheikh's horses, and there are a number of promising horses at Godolphin that motivate him to continue riding at the highest level.

Frankie is a jockey that comes along once in a lifetime, but the impact he has had on the sport of racing is immeasurable and entirely incomparable. Yes, every generation has its star jockey, and perhaps looking through history it is possible to argue that a very small number of others could match him for natural riding ability. But Frankie's charm, charisma and larger-than-life persona have taken his eminence to a level never held by any other jockey.

Wherever Frankie's future may lie, it's certain we haven't seen the last of him – he will not be fading into the background of public conscience anytime soon. This son of Italy, who, as a shy 14-year-old made Britain his home, has revolutionised racing, winning over the hearts of millions in the process. Frankie Dettori is far more than a jockey, a media personality and an entrepreneur – he is now a national institution.